Introduction

Do your teenagers attend Sunday school, only to leave before church starts? Do they attend youth events without ever meeting your senior pastor? Do some of them know nothing about what makes your church or your church's traditions distinctive? After confirmation, do your young people leave the church never to return?

We all want to make a lasting impression on our youth, to help them sustain a life-long relationship with the church. But because of their specific needs and challenges, it's easy to see teenagers as a specialized group, forgetting the importance of recognizing their valuable place in the church at large. One way to help youth feel connected to the church is to give them meaningful ways to participate. As teenagers exercise their gifts within the context of the church and build meaningful relationships with people in the church, they'll experience the body of Christ at its best.

This is a book of ideas for involving young people in the life of the church in meaningful ways. You'll find ideas that will help your young people connect with other generations in the church. You'll find ways for them to exercise their gifts and give their valuable input. And you'll even find creative ways to draw families together. The ideas fall into five categories: intergenerational activities, service ideas, church builders, family events, and ministry opportunities.

Intergenerational Activities are ideas to help teenagers interact with people in other age groups. For example, teenagers might help nursing home residents create memory books, spend a day teaching sports to the children in the church, or spend an evening having fun with adults.

Service Ideas are ideas to encourage teenagers to serve others in the church. For example, they might clean church offices, raise money to give away, or help senior adults with their gardening.

Church Builders are ideas to have teenagers participate in the administration and planning of the church. For example, teenagers might create a church brochure, propose a new ministry for the church, or evaluate vacation Bible school programs.

Family Events are ideas to pull families together and into the church. For example, teenagers might initiate a family conflict-resolution class, host an olympics of dumb games, or plan a day-long family retreat.

Ministry Opportunities are ideas to help teenagers use their spiritual gifts in the church. For example, youth might lead worship on a Sunday morning, form a clown troupe, or set up a prayer chain.

Each idea is identified as a low-investment , medium-investment , or high-investment idea. These investment levels indicate the amount of work, finances, or change required by you, teenagers, families, or your church. Some of the high-investment ideas may pay big dividends for your youth ministry and your church, but make sure you and your church are ready to make the investment before you begin! If you want to make a certain level of investment in an idea, check out the "Investment-Level Index" at the back of the book.

Try out the ideas in this book. You're sure to find some great activities and events that will work in your church to help your teenagers feel like a part of the church body. And you'll help them make connections that will last a lifetime!

No More
Us&Them

Group
Loveland, Colorado

No More
Us & Them

Credits
Contributing Authors: Tim Baker, Debbie Gowensmith, Michele Howe, Mikal Keefer, Jan Kershner, Burton Laine, Karl Leuthauser, Dennis R. McLaughlin, Lana Jo McLaughlin, Julie Meiklejohn, Janet Dodge Narum, Lori Haynes Niles, Pamela J. Shoup, Trevor Simpson, Cheryl B. Slater
Editor: Amy Simpson
Creative Development Editor: Jim Kochenburger
Chief Creative Officer: Joani Schultz
Copy Editor: Shirley Michaels
Art Director: Kari K. Monson
Cover Art Director: Jeff A. Storm
Cover Designer: Becky Hawley
Computer Graphic Artist: Desktop Miracles
Illustrators: Paula Becker and Amy Bryant
Cover Illustrator: Pam-ela Harrelson
Production Manager: Peggy Naylor

Library of Congress Cataloging-in-Publication Data
No more us & them.
     p. cm.
    Includes index.
    ISBN 0-7644-2092-5 (alk. paper)
    1. Church work with teenagers. I. Group Publishing. II. Title: No more us and them.
BV4447.N6 1999
259'.23—dc21

99-21489
CIP

10 9 8 7 6 5 4 3 2 1   08 07 06 05 04 03 02 01 00

Printed in the United States of America.

Contents

Introduction **9**

Intergenerational Activities **11**

Adopt-an-Adult 11
> Teenagers will adopt adults for an event of fun and fellowship.

Bringing the Bible to Life 11
> Teenagers will teach a Sunday school lesson to children.

Church Family Tree 12
> Youth will create a church family tree display in an area
> where it can be enjoyed by everyone.

Day Camp for Seniors 13
> Teenagers will plan and sponsor a day camp for seniors.

Finding Joy in Memories 14
> Teenagers will pair up with nursing home residents to create memory books.

Food-Drive Food Fair 16
> Youth will sponsor a food fair for the entire church to collect canned food.

Game Day at Sunday School 16
> Youth will host a time for the various generations in your church to play together.

Happy Birthday Club 18
> Students will create birthday cards for senior adults in your church.

Heritage Dinner 18
> Following a church dinner, youth will interview longtime members
> regarding church history and compile their answers in a publication that will
> help new and prospective members learn the history of the congregation.

Intergenerational Prayer Trios 19
> Teenagers will commit to pray with others in the church.

Muffins and Ministry 21
> Teenagers and seniors will share their concerns
> with each other and then pray about them.

Parent-Youth Court 23
> Teenagers, children, parents, grandparents, and single adults will role play a
> courtroom drama to help them see from one another's perspectives.

Reaching Around the Globe 24
> Teenagers will plan International Night for all ages at your church.

Roots of the Church 25
> Teenagers will interview "old-timers" in the church
> to compile a record of the church's history.

Secret Grandparent Pen Pals 26
Each teenager will receive a secret grandparent or set
of grandparents as pen pals, then they'll meet face to face.

Senior Appreciation Day 27
Students will create, develop, and implement a time of celebration
for the senior adults in their congregation or community.

Sponsoring New Members 28
Teenagers will sponsor adults to become new church members.

Sports Festival 28
Youth will host a festival to teach children the fundamentals of favorite sports.

Sunday Shut-In Picnics 29
Youth will commit to eating a picnic-style lunch with
a senior shut-in once a month during the school year.

When I Was Ten 31
Teenagers and families will interact with other age groups
at the church and get to know each other.

Service Ideas **33**
Adopt-a-Chore 33
Teenagers will assist church members who need help with chores.

Adopt-a-Fire Station 34
Youth will develop and carry out a plan to honor community servants.

Baby-Shower Power 34
Youth will host a baby shower to supply items for a local social service organization.

Bringing Church Services to Shut-Ins 35
Teenagers will record church services, make duplicate tapes,
and take them to shut-ins.

Camping Out 37
Teenagers will partner with siblings, parents, or younger friends in the
church to volunteer time and talents at a summer camp for the disabled.

Cleaning out the Cobwebs 37
Youth will clean and repair the church offices.

Crisis Response Team 39
Youth will make themselves available to help
church families in crisis or grieving situations.

Fifth-Sunday Worship Leaders 39
Youth will lead various aspects of the regular worship service
on the last Sunday of a month with five Sundays.

Mix-and-Match Canned Food Drive 40
Generations will work together to acquire food for people in need.

One-Day Apprenticeships 41
Teenagers will assist church staff in their work for a day.

One-Hour Gardeners 41
Teenagers will offer to help senior adults in your church with their gardening.

One-Mile Can Pickup 43
    Teenagers will pick up aluminum cans for a mile in every direction
    from the church to raise and donate money.

Recycle-Everything Day 43
    Teenagers will organize and implement a churchwide recycling program.

Road Show Fund-Raiser 44
    Teenagers will take a drama, music, or puppet ministry
    on the road to raise money for a church-related service project.

Spring Break Fun 45
    Teenagers will organize and run a day camp for children during spring break.

Surprise Sunday School Party 46
    Teenagers will encourage and thank people in your church by decorating
    classrooms, serving snacks, and praying for class members.

Walk for Hunger Relief 47
    Teenagers will plan a CROP Walk to raise money for world hunger relief.

Wash-a-Window 47
    Teenagers will wash windows of vehicles parked
    in the church parking lot during a church event.

Welcome Trees 48
    Teenagers will plant trees to welcome new families.

Whose Turf? 49
    Students will minister to adults by visiting them in their places of work.

Church Builders 50

Accounting Assistants 50
    One or two teenagers per week will participate with your church's
    offering counters and analyze income against need on a weekly basis.

Administration Days 50
    Teenagers will offer their enthusiasm and energy to support the church office staff.

Behind-the-Scenes Look 51
    Teenagers will learn what takes place behind the scenes of the church.

Big Stuff 52
    Youth will plan some big, important stuff in your church.

Church Anniversary Celebration 53
    Teenagers will take an active part in planning and
    celebrating a church anniversary or other historical occasion.

Church Brochure 53
    Youth will learn more about the church by creating a church brochure.

Comment Cards 55
    Teenagers will use a suggestion box to direct their comments,
    questions, and prayer requests to the staff of your church.

Community Connections 55
    Youth will serve as representatives to other youth programs in the community
    and will serve on a church program planning committee.

From the Ground Up 57
    Teenagers will research and propose a new ministry for their church, then take their
    idea through the proper administrative procedures to determine its viability.

Hot off the Press 58
    Teenagers will write, design, produce, and distribute the church newsletter.

Matching Grants 58
    Teenagers will actively support a ministry in your community, and
    your church will match their financial contributions to the ministry.

Mission-Board Minutes 59
    Youth will work with the missions committee to plan a churchwide missions meeting.

People Spotlight 60
    Students will organize and maintain a "People Spotlight" bulletin board.

Recruitment Lunch 61
    Teenagers will host a lunch to help recruit volunteers to teach Sunday school.

Research Assistants 61
    Teenagers will provide illustrations, video, multimedia,
    or other resources for the pastor's sermon.

Training Committee Chairs 63
    Youth will become involved in church committees after the
    committee chairs have been trained on involving youth.

VBS Evaluation 64
    Teenagers will evaluate advertisements for various VBS programs.

Web Page Proposals 65
    Teenagers will design a Web page for the church.

Youth Concerns Committee 66
    Generations will work together to help coordinate effective church programming.

Youth Evangelism Subcommittee 66
    Teenagers will form a subcommittee of the church outreach committee
    and develop a plan for telling other teenagers about Christ.

Family Events **68**

Adult Scavenger Hunt 68
    Teenagers will search the community for various types of adults.

Blended Families 69
    Teenagers will initiate a program that helps families of
    your church get to know each other better.

Building Families With Photographs 71
    Youth will organize family activities and document them with photographs.

Conflict-Resolution Class 71
    Teenagers will initiate a family conflict-resolution class.

Dumb-Game Olympics 72
    Teenagers will spend time in fun and zany fellowship with other generations.

Family Choir 74
    Teenagers will participate with their families in a choir for a specific worship service.

Family Crossword Swap 74
    Youth will work with their families to create crossword puzzles
    and then solve other families' crossword puzzles.

Family Heritage Festival 75
    Families will share their heritage with the larger church family.

Family Memories Night 75
    Students will organize an evening for families to talk about their family history.

Family Pride 76
    Families will create symbols to demonstrate who they are.

Family Progressive Dinner 77
    Families will host other families for a single course of a full meal
    and will share family traditions with their guests.

Family Retreat 78
    Teenagers will plan and help lead a day-long family retreat.

Family Summit 83
    Parents and teenagers will share youth group planning ideas and goals.

Grand-Slam Sleepovers 83
    A small group of families will "camp out" in the church to spend devotional time
    together, get to know each other, and cook up a church breakfast.

Holiday Memory Sharing 85
    Teenagers and their families will share special memories
    as part of a special holiday celebration.

Life Sports Small Groups 85
    Families will learn life sports together in a
    small-group setting that includes a Bible study.

Missions Mindset 87
    Teenagers will talk with their family members
    about supporting different missions organizations.

Secret Santa Stockings 88
    Working with their families, youth will stuff and
    deliver Christmas stockings to shut-ins and senior citizens.

Summer Movie Night 89
    Teenagers will plan and host a community family event on the church lawn.

Thanks, Mom and Dad 90
    Teenagers will create thank you cards for their parents.

Ministry Opportunities **92**
Advent Fair 92
    Teenagers will organize and lead an Advent fair for families.

Artistic Cover Design 93
    Teenagers will design covers for worship service bulletins or programs.

Fasting Prayer 94
    Youth will meet together during a meal time to fast and
    pray for an issue of vital concern to their church.

Invitation Cards 94
Teenagers will make printed cards to use in inviting other youth to Christian activities.

Just Clownin' Around 95
*Teenagers will organize and participate in a clown troupe to share God's message
with Sunday school classes, church organizations, and even the entire congregation.*

On Camera 96
Teenagers will form a video team to chronicle the life of the church family.

Pastoral Encouragement Team 97
Teenagers will work to encourage the senior pastor.

Pizza Box Calling Cards 98
*Teenagers will follow up with visitors to the church
by delivering gift certificates for pizzas.*

Prayer Chain 99
Youth will set up a prayer chain to let others know about midweek prayer concerns.

Prayer Visitors 99
Students will offer your church a gift of "prayer" for one month of church meetings.

Presenting Prayer 100
Teenagers will establish a regular time of prayer during the church's worship service.

Rugged Cross 101
*Youth will create a monument for the church
to serve as a reminder of God's incredible blessings.*

Sign-Along 102
*Teenagers will perform during the worship service by singing
and signing the words to one or more songs.*

Teaching Assistants 102
Teenagers will help teachers in children's Sunday school classes.

Teaching Confirmation 103
*After graduating from confirmation class, older youth
will help teach the next year's confirmation class.*

Those Were the Days 104
*Teenagers will use their own experiences to determine
how best to impact the kids in the church.*

Twenty-Four-Hour Prayer Vigil 105
*Teenagers will organize and participate in a
twenty-four-hour prayer vigil for the church.*

Visitation Teams 107
Youth will visit new teenagers who attend your church.

What God Is Doing 107
*Teenagers will create a video that demonstrates how
God has changed the lives of people in the church.*

Youth Prison Ministry 108
Generations will minister together to youth in prisons.

Investment-Level Index 110

Intergenerational
Activities

Adopt-an-Adult

Overview: Teenagers will adopt adults for an event of fun and fellowship.

Before this event, ask adults in your church to sign up for a specific evening to spend with teenagers. As adults sign up, make sure they know that the purpose of the event is for them to interact personally with teenagers rather than with other adults in their groups. Also explain that each person may have to spend up to five dollars. When you have enough adult volunteers, match each adult with a teenager of the same gender.

Tell teenagers which adults they'll adopt for a night of fun. Have each teenager pair up with another teenager, and explain that they'll be going out in groups of four (two teenagers and two adults). Before the evening, have the pairs of teenagers plan fellowship events for their groups of four. Encourage teenagers to make sure the event costs five dollars or less per person. If they have trouble coming up with ideas, you may want to suggest going out for dessert, playing putt-putt golf, bowling, or going to a lighted driving range.

On the night of the event, have the adults and teenagers meet at the church. Have teenagers connect with their "adopted" adults, and have groups of four begin their fellowship events. Make it very clear that groups must return to the church at a designated time. And be sure to give everyone a telephone number to call in case of emergency.

Bringing the Bible to Life

Overview: Teenagers will teach a Sunday school lesson to children.

Have your group plan a meaningful Sunday school lesson to teach to a class of children in your church. Teenagers can first choose an age level they'd like to teach for a day and then choose an appropriate Bible story or lesson. Children would enjoy seeing a story acted out by teenagers, so you may want to choose something appropriate for drama, such as the Last Supper, the feeding of the five thousand, or the story of Jonah and the big fish.

What will make the lesson meaningful for the children is the debriefing session that will follow the drama. Have teenagers plan questions beforehand to help children relate the Bible story to their own lives. Then during the lesson, have children gather in small groups of three or four for discussion led by the teenagers.

For example, after a skit on the story of Jonah, teenagers and children might discuss questions like these:

• How do we know what God wants us to do?

• Why is it hard sometimes to do what God wants you to do?

Teenagers may want to close the lesson with a snack that ties into the Bible story, such as fish-shaped crackers for the Jonah story.

Church Family Tree

Overview: Youth will create a church family tree display in an area where it can be enjoyed by everyone.

This activity is great because age really doesn't have much to do with the generations in this display of church history!

Using snapshots or pictures from your church directory, help teenagers create a family tree display. Mount a construction-paper trunk on a bulletin board or wall. Interview people to find out how long they've attended the church. Place the pictures of those who have attended the longest on the bottom branches and those who are

the newest attendees near the top.

If your church is quite established, determine which level people belong in by which decade they began attending the church. If your church is younger, place them by year. Don't forget to include new babies.

You may want to leave spaces within each "generation" and invite people to fill these spaces with photos of memorable occasions in the church. Each church's tree will take on a different shape, depending on when people became part of the fellowship. While some may look like pine trees, others will resemble a young oak with a narrow "trunk" and lots of new growth at the top. Let the youth combine their creativity to make the display uniquely theirs, adding design elements and title treatments to jazz it up.

Day Camp for Seniors

Overview: Teenagers will plan and sponsor a day camp for seniors.

Seniors will enthusiastically say, "We haven't done this in years!" when teenagers involve them in activities like cooking hot dogs or marshmallows over a campfire.

Assemble a team of teenagers who have interests both in camp counseling and in doing activities with seniors. Guide teenagers in choosing songs, games, and craft activities. The songs should be a balance of "old time" songs the seniors will know, hymns, and new camp songs that can be taught to them. The games should fit the activity level of the seniors. The craft activities can be traditional camp arts, such as working with leather, weaving, or painting rocks. It may be possible to do some simple heritage arts if there is a specific and common nationality background among church members. It would be even more fun if the crafts reflected diverse ethnicity.

Hold a training session for the teenagers ahead of time to teach them basic skills in leading activities and in working with seniors. Choose a location such as a public park with a shelter. Be sure to assign someone to coordinate meals and snacks at the day camp. Then have the counselors put together a schedule for the day camp. You may want to consider holding the day camp for three half-day sessions. This gives seniors and teenagers time to develop relationships without wearing themselves out.

The easiest way to gather a group of seniors is to promote the day camp among the seniors in your church. However, you may want to promote the event with flyers and possibly a personal invitation at area senior meetings. This may draw some unchurched seniors to the event.

Be sure teenagers know that they'll have to be flexible during the program. For example, they may want to have backup plans in case seniors don't seem to be enjoying themselves, and they may have to cut elements from the program if they run out of time. If your camp will last more than two days, after the first day, work together to assess the energy level and interests of the seniors who attended, and adapt the program for the following days as necessary.

Finding Joy in Memories

Overview: Teenagers will pair up with nursing home residents to create memory books.

Here's an idea that will give teenagers and seniors a chance to get to know one another better and will bring some real joy to the elderly.

Contact a local nursing home, explain the project, and get enough names of residents for all your teenagers to be paired up with someone. Be sure to explain that you'd like to take a photograph for the book, and find out if the nursing home requires a photo release from the resident's family.

Meet with teenagers before the scheduled nursing home visit. Tell them that they'll be putting together memory books for their partners. To do this, they should prepare a list of questions beforehand to get information to put in the book. Supply teenagers with notebooks and pens, and have everyone brainstorm about questions to ask and write these down before visiting the nursing home. Or if you can, give young people tape recorders so they can record their interviews and write up the details later.

Before this experience, you may want to encourage teenagers to practice interviewing grandparents or older church members so they have some idea what to expect.

Questions should be about birth place and date, childhood, family, work experiences, military experiences, favorite memories, favorite things, children and grandchildren, and interesting stories seniors might want to share. For example, teenagers might ask questions like these: What's a favorite childhood memory? Where did you go to school? How did you meet your spouse? How many children do you have? grandchildren? What kinds of work have you done? What hobbies have you enjoyed? What's your favorite place?

Suggest that teenagers use their general questions as a springboard for more specific questions. For example, when asking about children and grandchildren, youth can find out their names, ages, and where they live to list them in the book. A question about past careers can lead to details about that job. Asking about a favorite place can lead to questions about travels. Be sure teenagers know that some people will talk easily, while others may need more questioning.

Assign one or two people to be photographers (or do photography duty yourself). You may want to use an instant-print camera to save on film developing costs and time. When you go to the nursing home, have youth gather with their residents in a central area, such as a lobby or lounge, and spend at least thirty to sixty minutes with their partners to gather enough information for the memory books. Have adult volunteers circulate and help anyone who is having trouble gathering information. It's OK if the facts are vague if a teenager has a partner whose memories of the past aren't clear. In those cases, teenagers can focus on the person's favorite things, such as food, friends, or mementos. Teenagers will be creative enough to fill in gaps with other interesting things.

At your next youth meeting, supply construction paper, markers, colored pencils, pens, magazines, glue, tape, ribbon, doilies, and any other creative supplies for memory books. Have teenagers put together the stories of the people they interviewed in interesting ways and feature the photos prominently in the books. They might use a paper punch and ribbon to put the books together, or just staple the pages together. Have teenagers use creative drawings, decorations, or pictures from magazines to make the books look interesting and fun.

Once the books are compiled, arrange for another visit to the nursing home for presentation of the books to the residents. Allow enough time for teenagers to read the books to their partners and have a meaningful visit. These gifts will be cherished and shown off for a long time.

Food-Drive Food Fair

Overview: Youth will sponsor a food fair for the entire church to collect canned food.

The goal in this activity is for youth to collect canned food for the needy in their area. To collect the food, teenagers will plan an after-church fellowship meal for the entire church.

Divide youth into five teams. Each team will plan and make one portion of the meal. Team 1 will make vegetable dishes; Team 2 will make fruit dishes; Team 3 will make entrees; Team 4 will make desserts; and Team 5 will make drinks, set up the eating area, and clean up afterward.

Several weeks before the food fair, each team should meet and divide responsibilities. Invite the entire church by announcing the event in the bulletin, sending out handmade invitations, or hanging posters. Include the reason for the dinner (to bring in canned goods for the needy), the date, the time, the location, and the number of cans expected in exchange for the meal. For example, have adults bring three cans of food and children under twelve bring one can.

Teenagers should plan their dishes ahead of time and enlist the help of their families or other church members in preparing their food before the fellowship meal. Teenagers should also enlist the help of their families to entertain during the meal. Each family can be responsible for one five-minute song, skit, or reading.

Serve the dinner right after Sunday morning services. During the meal, announce when you'll be taking the food to the nearest food bank, soup kitchen, or other local support agency, and invite the entire church to go along.

Game Day at Sunday School

Overview: Youth will host a time for the various generations in your church to play together.

Here's a fun way to plant seeds of friendship among generations in your church. This event also can add excitement to the summer slump churches typically experience from Memorial Day through Labor Day.

Before this intergenerational activity, advertise the event in your bulletin or church newsletter. Youth may also want to design invitations for other Sunday school classes.

Have the youth invite the adults and children to a game day during the regular Sunday school time. Set up game centers in the fellowship hall or regular Sunday school classrooms. Assign a team of two or three youth to oversee each game center. The amount of space you have and the number of persons participating will determine the number of game centers, but a minimum of four centers is recommended. For game ideas, check out Group Publishing's *Gigantic Book of Games for Youth Ministry,* volumes 1 and 2.

One Church's Story

"We hosted 'Game Day at Sunday school' one July Sunday morning. It was great fun. We set up four different game centers (we have a small congregation) with folks ranging in age from three to eighty-three! One of our younger grandpas played Animal Match and Play-Doh with the nursery kids and preschoolers. Some of our ladies grouped with the elementary-age girls to play Bible Scramble. The most rowdy group was the boys and men who were playing Bible Baseball. We've never had so much laughter coming from our Sunday school area!

"We closed the time together with a giant prayer circle. It was great! The adults were all impressed with how much our kids knew about the Bible. I think I'll suggest we plan another game day next summer!"

Along with the game centers, you may want to set up a snack center where youth can serve cookies, donuts, fresh fruit, juices, or coffee to game day participants, either throughout the game time or during the last fifteen minutes.

As participants arrive, make play group assignments. Mix the children, adults, and any youth not operating game centers into groups of four to six persons. Be sensitive to smaller children who may be afraid to go with adults they don't know. Place them with their parents or older siblings. Give each group a fun name, such as an animal or a professional sports team.

Let each team choose a captain, who will make sure all group members travel together between centers, assist the game center leaders with demonstrations on how to play the games, and encourage all group members to play fair and have fun. Some game centers may require friendly competition among participants!

Each group may choose the game centers they wish to play in. Allow groups about fifteen minutes in each center. Then signal the end of the play period, and ask groups to switch centers.

Game day will lead to a spirit of unity and understanding that will overflow into other church activities.

Happy Birthday Club

Overview: Students will create birthday cards for senior adults in your church.

Ask your church secretary or pastor for the mailing addresses and birthdays of the senior adults in your church. Announce to the young people that you're going to spend the next year remembering the birthdays of the older people in your church. Then divide teenagers into the following two groups:

• **Card group**—This group must use the materials you provide to create the cards. Supply this group with card stock, markers, construction paper, and other supplies, such as glitter, glue, scissors, rulers, and stickers. Ask them to be sure to decorate appropriately for the age group.

• **Envelope group**—This group's job is to address the envelopes. Supply them with large envelopes, pens, and stamps. Remind the group to use large, neat penmanship and to be sure they get the addresses correct. Give groups as much time as they need to create and address the cards for all the birthdays in the next year.

When both groups have finished, gather everyone together and have them match cards with envelopes and seal the envelopes. Give the cards to a few responsible teenagers in the group, assigning them the responsibility of mailing the cards at the appropriate times throughout the year.

Heritage Dinner

Overview: Following a church dinner, youth will interview long-time members regarding church history and compile their answers in a publication that will help new and prospective members learn the history of the congregation.

Along with teaching our youth the history of God's chosen people and the early church as set forth in the Bible, it's important to pass along the spiritual heritage of their own congregation. Knowing the joys and disappointments of the past can help prepare and guide the church and its spiritual leaders into the future. Help teenagers honor the past and those who have faithfully served in your own congregation by hosting a heritage dinner.

Allow plenty of time and energy to prepare for and carry out this event. Invite the entire church to a special dinner: a potluck dinner, a catered dinner, or a dinner prepared by the youth and their leaders. Send special invitations to long-time members of the church, including a list of the questions youth will be asking. (See sample questions on p. 20.) Older members may need time to recall events of the past. Also encourage them to bring old pictures, newspaper articles, or scrapbooks they would be willing to display.

Youth should assist with the setup of tables and decorations. Also, have a crew ready to help with cleanup.

Following the dinner, youth will interview long-time members as a group about the beginnings of the congregation, how it has changed over time, and special memories of meaningful worship services, vacation Bible school programs, mission projects, and other events. Teenagers can take turns asking questions of the entire group, and the older members can volunteer to answer the questions they want to. A moderator should direct the interview to keep things flowing and make sure everyone has an opportunity to share. Have someone videotape and make a cassette recording of the interview.

One Church's Story

"At our heritage dinner, the teenagers were impressed to hear about the mission and outreach projects the older folks remembered from their youth. One of the agencies our older members worked to support when they were younger is also being supported by our youth today.

"Some of our older members told of riding their horses to Sunday school or coming to church in buggies. Some shared about the many Sunday school parties and picnics they remembered from their childhood. I think some of the teenagers were surprised to hear that these older folks like to have parties too!"

After the event, have the church computer expert(s) help youth transcribe the shared memories into a publication to be given to new or prospective church members. Be sure to photocopy or scan any old photos that would be of interest to readers.

Gathering and recording stories of the past may take a lot of time and energy, but it's worth it. Hearing of the sacrifices and acts of service given to bring the congregation into the present can ignite a new commitment to move with faith and trust into the future.

Intergenerational Prayer Trios

Overview: Teenagers will commit to pray with others in the church.

Announce to your teenagers that you'd like to set up intergenerational prayer

Questions for Heritage Dinner

- What do you know about our church's founder and/or first pastor?

- Do you know why and how our church was born?

- Can you share a favorite memory from your early years in this church?

- Can you tell us about programs or special projects carried out in this church many years ago?

- Which ministers do you remember most vividly and why?

- How did you travel to Sunday school and church?

- Who was your favorite Sunday school teacher? Why?

- Did you participate in vacation Bible school? Can you share any funny VBS memories?

- Did you attend youth group? What were some of your favorite youth programs?

- What are some ways you have served this congregation?

- What are some of the congregation's special spiritual gifts you are grateful for?

- How do you think the congregation today reflects the congregation of years ago?

- How or what has our congregation contributed to the community?

- What memories do you have of mission trips and projects?

- How has this church been able to nurture you in your own faith journey?

- When was this church building built? How much did it cost? How did we pay for it?

- Can you tell us about a particularly moving worship service you experienced in this church?

- What are your hopes for our congregation as we move into the future?

trios. Ask for volunteers who will commit to praying with other people in your church. Have all your teenage volunteers fill out the "Prayer Partners Needed" bulletin insert (p. 22) for your files.

Include the "Prayer Partners Needed" bulletin insert in your church bulletins a few weeks before you intend to begin having partners pray. Publicize the need for prayer partners with items in the church newsletter and announcements during your worship service and at Sunday school.

When you have enough volunteers available, match people in groups of three according to the times they're available. Be sure to mix generations as much as possible. If you have some people without partners, form groups of four as necessary. Then kick off your prayer groups by hosting a one-hour prayer event at your church. Invite prayer partners to come and spend time getting to know each other. Provide snacks and lead some crowd breakers; then spend some time in group prayer.

> **Tip**
>
> *It's a good idea to organize prayer partners in groups of three. Trios have the personal touch of a small group without the potential awkwardness of pairs.*

Instruct prayer partners to set up specific, regular times to meet for prayer in homes, over the phone, or in public places such as restaurants.

Muffins and Ministry

Overview: Teenagers and seniors will share their concerns with each other and then pray about them.

For an intimate time of prayer that will help your teenagers and seniors better understand each other, set up a prayer breakfast. Schedule the breakfast for about

Prayer Partners Needed

Do you like to pray?

Would you like to get to know other people who like to pray too?

The young people in our church are getting people together in groups of three to pray. We're looking for prayer partners of all ages.

The only requirement is that you must meet _____ times per month and pray for _____ minutes. If you're interested, fill in the appropriate information below and give it to _____.

Name _____.

Phone number _____.

The best time for me to meet and pray would be

_____.

The second best time would be

_____.

twenty minutes at a convenient time on Sunday morning—before or during Sunday school, for example. Have the teenagers and the seniors meet for juice, coffee, and muffins in a setting other than their regular Sunday school rooms. This will help prevent the segregated seating that occurs when people drift to their normal seats. To encourage teenagers and seniors to mix, ask them to sit with each other in groups of two teenagers and two seniors while they eat. Each person should have an opportunity to talk about his or her top three universal or personal prayer concerns.

After everyone has eaten, have small groups pray together. Encourage everyone to take a turn praying, and ask people to pray for concerns they heard others talk about during breakfast. After a few minutes of small-group prayer, ask several volunteers to talk to the whole group about some of the concerns.

Close the prayer breakfast with a minute or two or large-group prayer, asking God to address their concerns and to foster understanding among everyone in the church.

Parent-Youth Court

Overview: Teenagers, children, parents, grandparents, and single adults will role play a courtroom drama to help them see issues from one another's perspectives.

You may want to hold this event on a regular basis to foster healthy communication among generations. You can convene this court in a youth group meeting or any other appropriate church event.

Invite everyone in your church to participate in this event. Have families with teenagers work as teams, "adopting" into their families any people without family ties to a teenager. So a family might "adopt" a single adult, a set of grandparents, and a young couple with a baby. If you have teenagers whose parents aren't present, those teenagers can also adopt other people to form a family.

Work with teenagers to develop a list of issues that often bring about conflict between parents and youth. These might include curfews, driving, friends, clothing, and drinking. Assign each issue to a particular family group who will create a scenario about that issue. For example, if the Jones family is assigned the issue of curfew, they might come up with a story that on a given night Sarah Jones, a teenager, stayed out until 1:00 a.m. when her curfew was 11:00 p.m.

The parents of the teenager play the role of the prosecuting attorney; the teenager(s), the defendant; the youth leader, the defense attorney; another participant, the judge; and a mixed group of twelve is the jury. Parties on both sides of the issue can call witnesses. This is an important element of the event and will allow interesting insights from grandparents, younger siblings, and single adults.

At the end of the hearing, the jury can spend a few minutes deliberating and then present its verdict. With each new session, pick another jury and judge so everyone gets to participate.

Before the court session begins, assign a specific time limit—perhaps thirty minutes—for each family's issue. Have the parents begin by presenting their case and calling witnesses. In the case of a curfew violation, the parents might call witnesses to testify to how worried they were when Sarah didn't come home on time, or they might call on a parent who had a similar incident in which the outcome was disaster.

The defense attorney should follow by calling witnesses and leading the defendant (teenager) through a series of questions to bring out his or her side of the story. Grandparents might be called as witnesses for either side. For example, a grandparent might recall a time when the teenager's parent did the same thing. A single adult might be called to testify from a different perspective.

The more generations and participants you have, the more interesting and fun this activity will be. It can be as simple or as complex as you care to make it. Keep in mind, the intent is not to win the court case, but for all participants to come to a better understanding of each other, seeing life from one another's perspectives. Be sure to use humor and keep the event lighthearted.

Reaching Around the Globe

Overview: Teenagers will plan International Night for all ages at your church.

This event makes a great springboard for a missions project.

Plan an international night at your church, with your youth group coordinating the event. Have teenagers schedule the time and date, make invitations, and reserve a large room. Teenagers can invite the entire church to this event, but they should issue a specific invitation to each Sunday school class.

The invitations should instruct each class to choose a country to represent, study that country's needs, bring an ethnic dish representing that country, and encourage dressing up in ethnic clothing for the evening. Make it clear that families involved in multiple classes should bring only one or two dishes. Ask participants to label the food with the country it represents and the name of the dish. Have youth provide drinks, paper plates, napkins, cups, and plastic utensils.

The youth can decorate the hall with an international theme and even secure entertainment for the evening—perhaps ethnic dancers, drummers, or singers. If you use this event as a kickoff for a missions project, encourage classes to share missions needs of the countries they chose. At the dinner you might take an offering for a missionary family your church sponsors.

Allow teenagers plenty of time to plan the event and keep the publicity flowing in church and Sunday school classes. And have a video camera on hand to record the memories.

Roots of the Church

Overview: Teenagers will interview "old-timers" in the church to compile a record of the church's history.

Teenagers tend to focus on the here and now. This activity will help them expand their horizons a bit when it comes to thinking about their church and its history.

Teenagers will interview older members of the church, record their memories about the church, and possibly borrow photographs for this walk down memory lane. The project can be as simple as having each youth group member collect one story from the church's past, or the entire group might create a scrapbook, poster presentation, or video of their findings.

Have teenagers first check with church leadership for tips on who might provide a good starting place for the interviews. If teenagers borrow photos for this project, caution them to be very careful with the pictures. It might be wise to make high-quality color copies of the photos and return them to their owners right away.

Before teenagers get started, it might be wise for them to develop a standard list of questions. Suggested questions might include these:

• What special holiday memories do you have of the church?

• What's your funniest memory from church?

• Are there any special memories you have about building programs the church has undertaken?

• Do you have any memories to share about past church leaders or members?

Other starting points for questions and conversation could include weddings, children's programs, weather (significant storms in the past and their impact on the church), changes in the community, and changes in church doctrines and customs. Youth group members might become so intrigued with this project they may even want to track down former members and interview them by phone or mail. (Check with the church secretary for addresses of former members. Many like to stay in touch.)

To gain insight into how the church touches lives, teenagers might end each interview with the question, "When has this church had the most meaning or impact in your life?"

After teenagers have collected all their data, let the youth group decide how they want to present their findings to the church. They might create one scrapbook or poster to display in the foyer one Sunday, they may each present a verbal story, they might create a video, or they may even want to create a booklet to copy and distribute to church members. (Note: This could make a great fund raiser for your youth group, especially if it coincides with your church anniversary.)

Variation: If yours is a very young church, consider having teenagers interview members about their decision to come to your church. Have them ask members where they came from and what they especially like about your church.

Secret Grandparent Pen Pals

Overview: Each teenager will receive a secret grandparent or set of grandparents as pen pals; then they'll meet face to face.

To keep the initial secrecy between pen pals, the youth leader should coordinate this activity, setting up teenagers with senior congregational members who volunteer to be secret grandparents. Each grandparent or set of grandparents should be assigned a simple identification number or letter that corresponds to their pen pal. The teenager assigned to that set of grandparents should be given the same identification number, but neither party should be given the identification of their secret pen pals. The youth leader will be the only person who initially knows the identity of the teenagers and their secret grandparents.

Each week for a month, pen pals should write to each other, telling things about themselves without revealing their true identity. The letters should be signed only with the assigned identification numbers. It will be up to the youth leader to act as the mail coordinator and ensure that all mail is collected and delivered. One option for mail distribution is to set up mail slots or envelopes

> **Tip**
>
> When scheduling the social meeting, be sensitive to the transportation needs of the grandparents. Some of them may need transportation to and from the meeting. Also note that it is difficult for some senior adults to drive after dark.

in a central location in the church. The slots or envelopes can be labeled with the appropriate identification numbers, and people can drop their letters in the slots.

After a month of secret letter exchanges, schedule a social meeting of all the participating teenagers and secret grandparents. Begin the meeting by having each person try to guess the identity of his or her secret pen pal(s). Then have each teenager get into a small group with his or her grandparents. Have the grandparents share what life was like when they were teenagers. Then have the teenagers share some of the challenges and situations they face.

Senior Appreciation Day

Overview: Students will create, develop, and implement a time of celebration for the senior adults in their congregation or community.

This event may include a carnival, a formal dinner, public sharing and appreciation, service projects, or any other ideas that will show appreciation for the senior adults in your church or community.

Approximately one month before the intended party date, begin your preparation. Work with teenagers to assess how this event will work, where it will be, and what will it look like. Discuss how the group will work together in the next month to create a strong event. Then assign students to the following committees:

• **Publicity**—These committee members are responsible for informing the church and/or community about the event.

• **Food**—This group will plan the food. They may want to serve the food themselves, coordinate a potluck, or set up a buffet.

• **Setup and cleanup**—This committee will have to show up early to set up for the event and will clean up the party site afterward.

• **Transportation**—Many seniors in the community may not have their own transportation to the event. This committee will seek out shut-ins and establish a "taxi service" for those who need it.

• **Intergenerational integration**—This committee will recruit other generations to be a part of the program. Children, youth, young adults, and middle-aged adults should have opportunities to serve during this event.

• **Speaking/sharing**—This committee will schedule a speaker if needed or facilitate a guided public sharing time.

• **Activities**—This group will plan elements such as games, mixers, door prizes, and music to ensure a smooth flow and a festive atmosphere.

This activity should allow the entire congregation and/or community to applaud the importance of senior adults in our lives.

Sponsoring New Members

Overview: Teenagers will sponsor adults to become new church members.

Most churches have some process for sponsoring new members. During a church service, the sponsors may stand behind the new members at the altar and pledge support as they participate in the service.

When teenagers sponsor new members, they learn the value of living a Christian lifestyle. They see that they can make a lasting impact on others by helping them become part of a church. They realize that they can bring new skills into a church through the new members they sponsor. And they become more comfortable expressing their Christian faith publicly.

The first step can be to simply have a teenager and an adult member both stand behind a new member at a membership ceremony. This will model the procedure for the rest of the congregation. Then present the idea to all the young people in the church so they know they can be a part of bringing new members into the church.

Be sure to provide training for the youth so they know how people become church members. When participating as a sponsor, it's important to know exactly what will happen in the education process and the ceremony for the new members. It's also imperative to help teenagers understand the importance of following through on the commitments they're making so the new members will feel important and cared for.

Sports Festival

Overview: Youth will host a festival to teach children the fundamentals of favorite sports.

Encourage each teenager to identify a "sport" he or she is proficient at. (The sport could be balancing a flying disk on his or her nose!) Then have teenagers form groups with similar interests. Let each group decide on one or more fundamentals they believe they could teach to children from kindergarten to fifth or sixth grade.

Plan a day when your student athletes can host the children in your church to teach these basic skills. List each of the group's skill areas on the "Score Card" (p. 30), and make photocopies for the children who will participate. The day of the event, set up skill areas all around your facility along with a water and snack station manned by anyone in your youth group who doesn't feel comfortable teaching a sport skill.

As children go from place to place learning skills from the youth, have the youth sign off on their score cards. Children will love the variety of activities and the individual attention of the youth. End the festival with a quick devotion based on 2 Timothy 2:5—"Similarly, if anyone competes as an athlete, he does not receive the victor's crown unless he competes according to the rules"—or another passage that connects to athletic endeavors.

Sunday Shut-In Picnics

Overview: Youth will commit to eating a picnic-style lunch with a senior shut-in once a month during the school year.

This activity requires a full school-year commitment of one Sunday afternoon a month. Before you establish this program, make sure you have youth who are willing to make this kind of long-term commitment.

Determine which Sunday of each month you'll plan the shut-in picnic. Arrange for families in the church to agree to provide a three-person picnic lunch for those days so teenagers won't have to worry about preparing food.

Make a list of the senior shut-ins who are willing to participate in this activity, identifying an adult liaison from your church for each one. Assign two teenagers to each senior. (It helps if at least one of the partners can provide transportation.) Have the pair meet with the adult liaison to learn about their shut-in prior to the first visit. On the first visit, the liaison should accompany the youth to make the introductions.

Plan for a roster of "substitutes" in your group from those who can't commit to a full school year of monthly visits but would still like to be involved. If one of your committed visitors is unable to keep his or her appointment, that person should find a substitute from the list, as the shut-ins will come to count on the monthly visits. Be sure to remind everyone the week before each Sunday shut-in picnic to prevent disappointments.

After church on the designated Sundays, have the adult picnic providers and youth visitor teams meet in a predetermined location to hand off the lunches and

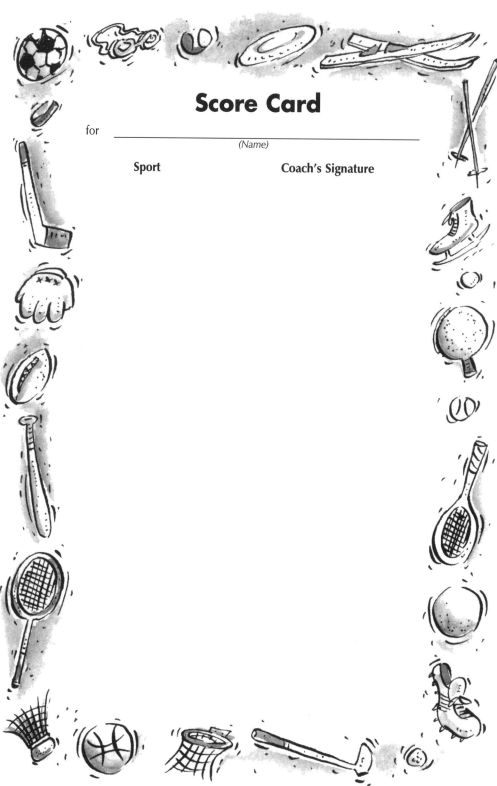

Score Card

for _____
(Name)

Sport   **Coach's Signature**

to pray together for the visits. It may be helpful to provide some conversation starters for your visitors each month, as well. Try these:

- Tell us about the house you lived in when you were a child.
- What were your kids like when they were teenagers?
- What pets have you had?
- What are your favorite memories of church?

After young people have visited for several months, have them add suggestions to the list of conversation starters based on successful visits they've had with their shut-ins.

Don't be afraid to start small with this project. Enthusiasm will build as people see how valuable the connection between youth and seniors can be.

When I Was Ten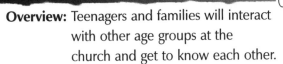

Overview: Teenagers and families will interact with other age groups at the church and get to know each other.

Your youth can help build relationships in your church with this simple, entertaining event. Everyone loves a good story, so arrange a celebration at which people share life stories. You'll prompt family storytelling that draws families closer and helps people in your congregation connect with each other.

Ask families in your church to come to an ice-cream potluck. A simple way to make sure you end up with something besides chocolate topping is to ask families whose last names begin with A-K to bring their favorite ice cream and families whose last names begin with L-V to bring favorite toppings. The W-Z people get to just come; they've had a hard life—always being at the end of the alphabet—and deserve a break.

Phone ten key members of the congregation—including teenagers—well *before* the meeting and ask them to speak for three minutes each on the theme "When I was ten…"

Keep in mind that the fear of public speaking runs rampant, so you may have to cajole and beg. Be persistent! You'll need a wide range of ages and backgrounds.

Explain that you'll provide the world background, so you want speakers to talk about *themselves*, not the world in general. For starters, you might suggest that speakers answer the following questions: Where were you living? What was your favorite game? Did you go to church? Where? What did you study in school? What was the latest, greatest invention?

As delicately as possible, try to find out the year the person was ten. You'll need that information for your research and development team. (Note: Don't believe that only women are sensitive about their ages. Men are just as likely to balk about giving you specific dates. Again, be persistent!)

You'll need three teams to pull this off:

• **Research and Development**—This team will hit the library or the Web to find out what was happening in specific years. What was life like? Who was president? How much did a loaf of bread cost? What was in the news? Be ready to introduce each speaker with a thirty-second summary of this information.

• **Q&A**—Have the Q&A team develop a list of at least thirty questions, one for each day of the month, that families can discuss at the dinner table. They should write questions that are open-ended and prompt memories. An open-ended question is one that can't be answered "yes" or "no" or with one word. For example, rather than "Did your mom and dad ever punish you?" ask, "What's something you did that got you in trouble with your mom and dad?" This team must have the questions written, edited, printed, and ready for distribution at the ice-cream potluck.

• **Mop and Bucket Brigade**—Hey, ice cream is messy. Church janitors are known to be armed. You figure it out.

Advertise this event well in advance and ask for RSVPs to help you plan. But be flexible—welcome anyone who comes. And have extra bowls and spoons available at all times!

As the event begins, place a stool where everyone can see it while they're eating their ice cream. Encourage young children to gather on the floor near the stool. Proximity will keep them focused, and the little faces will help speakers remember to include the children. Introduce each speaker with a brief background on the appropriate year, and lead applause as each speaker finishes. Keep the entire program at about forty-five minutes total. Mix up the ages you present, but leave the oldest participant until last.

When the formal program has ended, if you have extra time, encourage anyone who wishes to share a story about when they were ten. Ask especially for stories that tell what the storyteller thought about God at the time.

As people leave, distribute Q&A sheets for people to discuss at home.

Service Ideas

Adopt-a-Chore

Overview: Teenagers will assist church members who need help with chores.

For a parent with a sick child, someone with a broken leg, or a teenager with a car in the shop, even simple chores and errands are stressful. Your teenagers can help by creating an adopt-a-chore program.

Here's how the program works: When someone needs help, he or she calls the program's contact person. The contact person asks for a name and phone number, what needs to be done, how long it might take, and how many people it might require. Then the contact person checks a list of teenagers' names and calls the next two people in line. Those teenagers are then responsible for scheduling the chore with the person who needs help. Be sure to send two teenagers to do a chore. They have company, and they're safer.

Have teenagers who are willing to commit several hours a month to the program sign up. Talk with those teenagers about the kinds of chores they might be doing, such as mowing lawns, delivering groceries, or cleaning rooms. Make sure teenagers understand that they won't be paid for the work they do and that you won't ask them to do unrealistic chores, such as paint houses and landscape yards. For fairness, have teenagers write their names on slips of paper, then draw their names from a hat. List their names in the order you draw them from the hat, and explain that they'll be "hired out" in that order on a rotating basis.

Ask a mature, organized teenager—someone who can delegate—or an adult volunteer to be the contact person for the program. This person will receive calls from people who would like help, gather information from the caller, and then pass the information to the teenagers whose turn it is to help.

Next, present the program to your congregation during a worship service, in bulletins and newsletters, or on the church's Web page. It's essential that you present the program accurately, including its limitations. Explain that the program isn't a substitution for paid maid service; it's a service the teenagers are offering to people in difficult circumstances. Give examples of the work your teenagers can do and can't do to avoid unrealistic expectations. Also emphasize that while teenagers won't accept any payment for their work, they won't be able to purchase the groceries they deliver or the gasoline used to mow the lawn.

To get the program started, write or call people whose names are on your church's prayer list. Also talk with church leadership about people to contact. Your teenagers will be in high demand in no time!

Adopt-a-Fire Station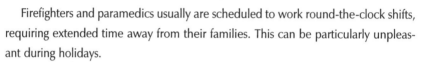

Overview: Youth will develop and carry out a plan to honor community servants.

Firefighters and paramedics usually are scheduled to work round-the-clock shifts, requiring extended time away from their families. This can be particularly unpleasant during holidays.

Have the group brainstorm about some specific stresses of these community servants. Or you might even encourage your group to do some research together, interviewing the chief or one of the department chaplains.

Form small groups to search out ways to communicate support for these people. Ask each group to devise an action plan, complete with a proposed time line and budget, if necessary. Let the groups share their plans, and have the whole group vote on a support plan they feel they can carry out. Encourage both creativity and feasibility as the youth work through this process. Once your group has come up with a plan, have them present the plan to the rest of the church and invite them to join the group in reaching out to the community servants.

One youth group organized a plan to provide enough cookies for each firefighter and paramedic on duty to take home to his or her family Thanksgiving Day. They returned two weeks later to carol. Later, they baked pies for Christmas dinner and gave the firefighters and paramedics coupons to their next car wash. This blitz allowed the church to really reach out to the station house that served their particular area of the community.

Baby-Shower Power

Overview: Youth will host a baby shower to supply items for a local social service organization.

Help teenagers plan and promote a "baby shower Sunday," inviting the whole church to participate in bringing baby shower items on a designated date. Publicize the event in your church bulletin (see the "invitation" on p. 36), through posters, and in any other publication your church presents. Ask adult Sunday school classes to allow teenagers to make personal announcements. In your publicity, include the list of suggested items on page 36.

Keep the event simple by serving blueberry muffins and pink punch as people come into the church. Collect the items in borrowed baby buggies, strollers, cribs, or playpens. Arrange to have a stroller parade with the collected items before, during, or after worship.

After the shower, arrange to donate the items to a local social service organization that reaches out to new parents.

Bringing Church Services to Shut-Ins

Overview: Teenagers will record church services, make duplicate tapes, and take them to shut-ins.

Shut-ins often feel separated from the community and may not have many visitors. For the purposes of this project, shut-ins can be handicapped persons, the elderly, or those without access to transportation and who can't easily get to church services. In any community, only one or two churches may have services broadcast on a radio or television station. Shut-ins can benefit greatly from the opportunity to listen to their own church service on audiocassette or watch a church service on videotape. They may benefit even more from having teenagers visit them weekly and bring them the tapes.

In deciding whether to make audio or video recordings of church services, consider the equipment available to shut-ins. The church may need to provide either a cassette player or a VCR with the tapes each week.

Also be sure youth have duplicating equipment available for making copies of church services. You can record over the tapes every other week to save on costs of buying new tapes.

Teenagers can be responsible for taping the services, duplicating the tapes, and visiting the shut-ins weekly. You may want to form teams of two or more teenagers for each shut-in so they can take turns doing the taping and visiting every other week.

It's a baby shower!

Date: _____

Place: _____

Time: _____

For: _____

Suggested items to bring

Baby brush and comb

Baby nail clippers

Baby shampoo

Baby soap

Baby wipes

Booties or socks

Bottles or bottle liners

Caps

Diaper cream

Disposable diapers

Pacifiers or teething rings

Receiving blankets

Small baby toys

Camping Out

Overview: Teenagers will partner with siblings, parents, or younger friends in the church to volunteer time and talents at a summer camp for the disabled.

Most areas of the country have summer camps for mentally or physically disabled children or adults. Locate a camp in your area, and find out if you can bring a group to help for a day or more as counselor aides or recreational leaders. If you don't have such a camp close by, check into helping out at your denomination's church camp instead.

To involve other church members in this service project, have each teenager bring at least one sibling, parent, younger friend from church, or grandparent to volunteer as a team.

Once you find a camp and know what age you'll be working with, have the group spend a meeting or two planning activities to share. For example, they might put on a show with music or skits, incorporating worship songs or a devotional activity (if permission is given from the camp). Other ideas would be to plan games or crafts suitable for people with disabilities or in wheelchairs. Be sure to give your camp contact a detailed explanation of your plans.

Here are some Group Publishing resources that might help in the planning: *Fun & Rowdy, Hilarious Skits for Youth Ministry, Fun & Easy Games, On-the-Edge Games for Youth Ministry, Goof-Proof Skits for Youth Ministry,* and *The Group Songbook.*

This could become an annual service project for your teenagers.

Cleaning out the Cobwebs

Overview: Youth will clean and repair the church offices.

Have teenagers send a letter to your church staff, requesting a date when they can spend several hours making repairs and cleaning church offices. The letter should include a list of chores the youth are skilled enough to perform. (See p. 38.) Ask the office staff to check off each chore they would like to have done and fill in others not listed.

Once a date has been set, have youth look over the list and divide into teams to do certain chores. Each team should be responsible for bringing in the necessary cleaning supplies.

Be sure everyone has a ride to the church on the designated date and brings a sack lunch for break time.

Chore Checklist

Please read through this list of chores, and check off the ones you would like us to do. Add any chores not listed.

❏ Sweep carpeting

❏ Clean carpeting

❏ Sweep hard floors

❏ Mop floors

❏ Sweep upholstery

❏ Spot-clean upholstery

❏ Dust furniture/knickknacks

❏ Polish lamps

❏ Dust ceilings for cobwebs

❏ Wash windows

❏ Wash window sills

❏ Clean window blinds

❏ Clean out garbage cans

❏ Wash walls

❏ Wash ceiling

❏ Clean bathrooms

❏ Organize closets

❏ Clean refrigerator

❏ Defrost freezer

❏ Other _____

Crisis Response Team

Overview: Youth will make themselves available to help church families in crisis or grieving situations.

When a family is grieving or facing a crisis, there are some skills youth can provide to help the family feel God's grace through the church. If it's a family with small children, youth can volunteer to baby-sit. Older youth can volunteer to housesit when there is a funeral or a family member is unexpectedly in the hospital. If the situation has been publicized in the newspaper or mentioned at a church service and it's likely that the house will be left empty, there may be concern about burglary of an untended home.

The first step is to work with your group to come up with a list of needs people in crisis situations might face. Then list the skills of youth in the church that could serve those needs. For example, teenagers might baby-sit, housesit, care for pets, provide meals, pick up mail, or gather prayer support.

Compile a list of willing volunteers and their skills, and give the list to the church secretary, a volunteer youth leader, or a responsible student who can coordinate the program. When a family faces a crisis situation, the family or someone aware of their needs can call the program coordinator for help. The coordinator will then call on the teenagers who can meet the needs of the family.

It may be necessary, depending on the skills of the youth, to provide training for helping out in a family home during specific circumstances. In some cases it may be necessary to team adults with youth for safety reasons.

Fifth-Sunday Worship Leaders

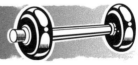

Overview: Youth will lead various aspects of the regular worship service on the last Sunday of a month with five Sundays.

This idea may become a meaningful tradition not only for youth, but for your entire church.

Check with your pastor or worship leader to determine which responsibilities in the service youth can carry out. For example, they may present the greeting, announcements, and call to worship; read Scripture; lead a responsive reading; pray the offering prayer; give the children's message; or sing.

Ask for volunteer teenagers, and meet with the participants a week before the worship service. Run through the order of worship, and have youth practice their parts. The day before the service, have them practice using the sound system. Encourage them, help calm any nerves, and pray with them.

Before the service, pray with the teenagers, and make sure they're in their places several minutes before the service begins. During the service, sit where teenagers can see your encouraging smile, and pray for their confidence and clarity of speech. Even the most outgoing young person can become weak-kneed or tongue-tied in front of the congregation.

This act of service requires courage, patience, and understanding from all those involved. Youth will gain a greater understanding of what it means to worship together and the roles of worship leaders. And your congregation will be blessed by the teenagers' gifts of service.

Mix-and-Match Canned Food Drive

Overview: Generations will work together to acquire food for people in need.

This event—designed to collect a lot of food in only a couple of hours—works great as a Halloween alternative.

During a time of intergenerational interaction (such as after church or at a midweek meeting time), have a canned food drive for the church food pantry or a local soup kitchen. Have the church consider matching the number of cans that are brought in by donating a set price for each can collected. For example, if three hundred cans are brought in and the church agrees to pay fifty cents per can, the group would raise $150 plus three hundred cans for the food pantry or a local soup kitchen.

During the canned food drive, have individuals and families form teams of ten to fifteen people. Encourage a wide variety of ages on each team if possible. After teams are established, give each team a map of the area and an assigned part of the community to solicit for cans. This will prohibit annoying overlapping for your neighbors.

One Church's Story

"When our church tried this idea, the youth generated enough food in forty-five minutes to make a difference at their local food bank. They laid out all the food in one place, and the teenagers enjoyed the immediate visual affirmation of their work!"

Give each team a stack of cards for residents that give an accurate description of your group and the cause you're collecting cans for. Then instruct each team to go out into the community and collect canned goods from neighboring homes. Have each team report back to the church at a specific time to turn in their cans and have them counted.

When all the cans are counted, you may want to have an informal award ceremony, giving out silly awards to teams with funny stories, positive testimonies, and the most can production. After you've counted all the cans and given out awards, announce the number of cans God has provided for those in need.

One-Day Apprenticeships

Overview: Teenagers will assist church staff in their work for a day.

Help your youth understand the work that goes on behind the scenes of your church by allowing them to share their time, energy, and skills with the church staff through an "apprenticeship" service project.

First, set your date for the one-day apprenticeships. A day during spring break or summer vacation or another day off from school will work better than a Saturday.

Next, send "Work Orders" (see p. 42) to all church staff. Ask staff members to list tasks teenagers might help them with on a typical day. Then match your young apprentices with staff members based on the tasks listed.

On the day of the apprenticeships, begin your workday in prayer with youth and staff members together. Throughout the day, periodically check in with teenagers and staff members to make sure everything is going smoothly.

Through their apprenticeship experiences, teenagers will gain an understanding of the day-to-day responsibilities of the church staff. They'll also see how the different parts of the body of Christ work together as one to carry out the church's mission.

One-Hour Gardeners

Overview: Teenagers will offer to help senior adults in your church with their gardening.

Ask for volunteer teenagers willing to help senior adults in your church with their weeding and light gardening. When you have teenagers who can help, inform the seniors in your church that the group of teenagers is willing to help them with their

Work Order

Our teenagers would like to donate their time and energy as one-day apprentices for church staff. Please fill out this form to help us match apprentices with staff people.

Staff Person's Name_____

Location/Room_____

Describe some of your tasks for a typical workday that a teenager could help you with:

_____

_____

You provide the supplies for the job, and the youth will supply the energy!

Work Order

Our teenagers would like to donate their time and energy as one-day apprentices for church staff. Please fill out this form to help us match apprentices with staff people.

Staff Person's Name_____

Location/Room_____

Describe some of your tasks for a typical workday that a teenager could help you with:

_____

_____

You provide the supplies for the job, and the youth will supply the energy!

gardening. Let them know the date and times students will be available, and have them sign up.

Begin by dropping off teenagers at the homes of people who have asked for help. Inform homeowners that you'll be picking up the teenagers in about one hour. Be sure seniors know that the teenagers shouldn't receive any payment for their work.

When the event is over, talk with teenagers about how they felt serving people in their church, what were the most difficult tasks, and whether they'd be willing to do the activity again.

One-Mile Can Pickup

Overview: Teenagers will pick up aluminum cans for a mile in every direction from the church to raise and donate money.

You'll need large plastic trash bags for this event, as well as adult transportation for each group.

Have teenagers form groups of three or four. Give each group two large trash bags. Explain that each team will be taken one mile from the church in a different direction. The object is for each group to work its way back to the church, picking up aluminum cans and other trash along the way. Instruct teams to put aluminum cans in one bag and other trash in the other bag.

When groups have been dropped off, the adult in charge of transportation should periodically check on his or her group members and make sure they keep their course. Assign someone to be in charge of cashing in the cans. (Many supermarkets and beverage distributors accept recycled aluminum cans.)

> **Tip**
>
> If your church is surrounded by heavily wooded areas, severe traffic, or other hazards, consider taking the teenagers to local parks for the same purpose.

After the cans have been turned in, challenge the group to decide how to spend the money. If the funds collected for this project are minimal, consider putting them into a holding fund. Then think of other ways to continue adding to it until the fund is substantial enough to donate to the group's ministry of choice.

Recycle-Everything Day

Overview: Teenagers will organize and implement a churchwide recycling program.

Do some good for your community, and help your church gain a sense of social responsibility by organizing a church recycling day.

Organize your students into the following teams.

• **Organization liaisons**—These students are responsible for contacting recycling organizations to check for specific packing and delivery requirements for various types of recyclable materials.

• **Transportation crew**—These students are responsible for transporting the materials to the various recycling centers. They must have reliable vans or trucks.

• **Recycling day coordinators**—These students will be the event's contact people. On the day of the event, these students will tell people where to place their goods. These students must also give an accurate account of the number of recycled materials to the congregation.

Have students choose various items to recycle, such as aluminum, clothes, plastic, paper, and automobile tires. Be sure to advertise the event to your church and community.

Ask groups to make signs that will designate material drop-off locations. If it works for your church, keep the event outside. Arrange drop-off locations with plenty of room for large piles and possible large crowds.

On the day of the event, ask students to show up one hour early. When everyone has arrived, begin the day with a short prayer, asking God to bless your efforts. After the event, place an announcement in your church newsletter, informing your congregation how much stuff you recycled.

Road Show Fund-Raiser

Overview: Teenagers will take a drama, music, or puppet ministry on the road to raise money for a church-related service project.

Encourage your teenagers to share the message of Christ with others around your city and even your state with a traveling drama, music, or puppet ministry.

Have teenagers identify a service project connected with your church, such as a missionary family, a food pantry or soup kitchen, a building need, a family trying to meet medical bills, or some other project, and have them "pass the hat" for donations for their project at each performance. Make this an ongoing fund-raiser for your youth group.

Start by having teenagers identify various talents within your group and discuss how they might use these talents in sharing their faith with others. They might write a drama or puppet show or explore Christian bookstores for material that is already published. If they choose already published material, be sure to check copyright and permissions for church use.

Musically inclined groups might prepare a concert or form a band to travel and perform. Really inspired groups may combine forms of ministry, such as drama and music. This will take a big commitment from your group and other church members for props, costumes, and transportation, plus many hours of rehearsal time. Make a special effort to involve parents or younger children in the church. Once your show is ready to be performed, start by contacting other local youth groups and asking to perform for them.

If the response is good and the teenagers are inspired, branch out to community groups or youth organizations, and take the show on the road!

Spring Break Fun

Overview: Teenagers will organize and run a day camp for children during spring break.

Spring break can be a difficult time for working parents with young children. Your teenagers can provide opportunities for learning and fun in a safe environment.

First, decide with your teenagers if you want to have an all-day camp or a half-day camp. Next, have teenagers sign up for the following teams:

Crafts—This team will find fun, easy craft ideas for children to do. Group Publishing has many excellent crafts resources, including *More Than Mud Pies* and *Bible-Time Crafts Your Kids Will Love.*

Games—This team will find exciting games for kids to play. Check out Group Publishing's game resources, including *Fun & Easy Games* and *Friend-Makers and Crowdbreakers.*

Outdoor Activities—This team will create fun outdoor activities, such as nature hikes and pool parties. Some good resources include *The Kids' Nature Book: 365 Indoor/Outdoor Activities and Experiences* (Williamson Publishing) and *Classic Outdoor Games* (Klutz Press).

Fun Trips—This team will arrange day trips. Some possibilities might include a trip to a zoo, a trip to an amusement park, or a horseback-riding trip.

Learning Activities—This team will create enriching activities to help children learn more about Jesus and the world they live in. Some great resources from Group

Publishing are *"Show Me!" Devotions for Leaders to Teach Kids* and *The Children's Worker's Encyclopedia of Bible-Teaching Ideas*.

Service Projects—This team will think of some meaningful projects kids can do to help others. One great resource is *Hands-On Service Ideas for Children's Ministry* (Group Publishing).

Snacks (and lunch if you choose an all-day format)—This team will provide the yummy "fuel" that will keep kids going!

One Church's Story

"Our youth hold this spring-break camp every year. Last year, at the end of the week a young single mom approached the youth director nearly in tears because her six-year-old had gotten so much out of the program. She was so excited, in part because she couldn't afford to leave her child in day care that whole week. Later, she became an active volunteer in the youth ministry."

After teenagers have signed up for teams, work with them to create a budget, a schedule, and a plan for locations. Then let them work in their teams to come up with ideas, purchase supplies, put the camp together, and run the camp. You'll probably want to recruit adult helpers to keep things running smoothly.

Surprise Sunday School Party

Overview: Teenagers will encourage and thank people in your church by decorating classrooms, serving snacks, and praying for class members.

Have youth meet at your church the night before your regular service. Give teenagers streamers, newsprint, markers, and balloons to decorate each classroom. Encourage teenagers to write messages of encouragement and thanks on sheets of newsprint and tape them to the walls. For example, they could write things like "We can't wait until you're in the youth group" in the fifth and sixth grade classroom or "You're a great example for us" in an adult classroom. Teenagers could also write encouraging and inspiring Scripture passages. The next day, bring snacks for all the Sunday school classes.

During Sunday school classes, have all the teenagers visit each room with the snacks. (You may want to make sure the teachers are aware of the surprise first!) After the teenagers have given the snacks to the class, announce that the youth want to say a prayer of blessing over the class members.

Direct teenagers to spread out among the class members and form small groups. Make sure each class member is in a group with a teenager. Have the teenagers pray a prayer of blessing and thanksgiving.

Thank the leader for allowing the interruption, and let him or her know that the teenagers will return after class to clean up the room. Continue this process for each class. When classes are over, have teenagers clean up the decorations and trash.

Walk for Hunger Relief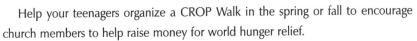

Overview: Teenagers will plan a CROP Walk to raise money for world hunger relief.

Help your teenagers organize a CROP Walk in the spring or fall to encourage church members to help raise money for world hunger relief.

CROP is sponsored by Church World Service to assist in disasters and famines, to help meet special needs of refugees, to support long-term development in more than seventy countries, and to support local hunger-fighting efforts across the United States. Since 1946, Church World Service has provided $879 million in food and material assistance for relief efforts around the world.

To obtain information on CROP, call toll-free 1-888-297-2767 for the regional office nearest to you, or visit their Web site (bruno.ncccusa.org/cws/crop.html).

Up to four weeks prior to the CROP Walk, have teenagers make an announcement (or present a skit) in church to explain CROP and encourage involvement of all ages in the church as walkers or sponsors. Teenagers should set up a table after church services over the next few weeks to sign up walkers and sponsors. CROP will send pledge envelopes and sign-up sheets, publicity materials, and even T-shirts.

On the day of the CROP Walk, have walkers gather in the church with a send-off from the pastor or from a church musical group. When everyone returns to the church, offer fruit, cookies, and drinks that teenagers can secure as donations from local merchants or church members.

Wash-a-Window

Overview: Teenagers will wash windows of vehicles parked in the church parking lot during a church event.

During a church event in which members' vehicles are parked in the church parking lot, divide the teenagers into groups of two or three. Provide the groups with window cleaning supplies and printed notes with a message such as "This car window washed compliments of the First Church Youth Group." Send groups out to wash all the car windows in the parking lot. After the windows of a vehicle are clean, have the group leave a copy of the note under one of the windshield wipers.

If traffic is heavy in the parking lot, station some adult helpers at each entrance to help with safety concerns.

Be sure to challenge the teenagers to do quality work as a way of demonstrating their commitment to Christ by serving others.

Welcome Trees

Overview: Teenagers will plant trees to welcome new families.

The growth of a church is exciting! Involve your teenagers in the joy and excitement by planting trees as a welcome to new members.

You'll need a section of your church property where you can plant the trees over time. Choose trees indigenous to your area, and plan where the trees will be planted.

When a new family joins your church, have teenagers plan a short but special ceremony to honor them. Include the planting of a tree in the ceremony, and explain how the growth of the tree symbolizes growth in faith and in the church family.

Encourage the families to look for their trees in the future and note how they're growing. You might want to give families their own trees to plant at home as well to serve as reminders of their growth and commitment.

Whose Turf?

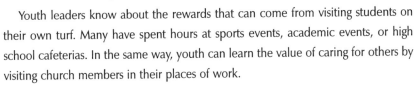

Overview: Students will minister to adults by visiting them in their places of work.

Youth leaders know about the rewards that can come from visiting students on their own turf. Many have spent hours at sports events, academic events, or high school cafeterias. In the same way, youth can learn the value of caring for others by visiting church members in their places of work.

Begin by studying 3 John 1-8 with your group. Take some time to explore these questions:

- Do people in our church feel your love for them?
- How do you think people in the church see us?
- How do they know we care about them?

Have teenagers make small gifts to take on friendly visits. You might try making little potted plants or small packages of cookies. Add a friendly card signed by some or all of the youth.

Then choose a convenient afternoon, and take youth to visit businesses and shops that employ some of your church members. (You may need to call some places in advance.) This is a particularly nice gesture for business owners. You can be assured that they'll welcome such a kind visit from smiling teenagers.

Make sure teenagers are instructed to deliver the gifts and leave after a minute or two. However, if church members ask teenagers to visit or take a tour, encourage them to stay for a few minutes. These visits can build lasting relationships.

Just think of the relationships you've built by visiting teenagers on their own turf. Your youth will be amazed at how honored your church members will be when teenagers visit them in the same way.

Church Builders

Accounting Assistants

Overview: One or two teenagers per week will participate with your church's offering counters and analyze income against need on a weekly basis.

With the approval of your church leaders, arrange for one or two teenagers to shadow the team that counts offering on Sunday mornings. Be sure to plan ahead to ensure that you observe your church's policy about anonymity in giving. Prepare the team to respect the sensitivity of the financial issues of the church.

Provide data about how much money your church needs each week to meet its budget. Have the youth do a weekly analysis of giving versus budget and create a graph that provides a visual picture of the church's financial health. The graph need not represent actual figures. It can show proportion of giving to need or trends over a specific length of time. (Make sure that other sources of income besides the Sunday offering are accounted for.)

Have teenagers keep track of income versus budget for several months before compiling their graph. When the graph is complete, have them share it with the entire church.

This experience can help youth understand the importance of faithful financial stewardship, clarify how the church actually spends income, and take some of the mystery out of what actually goes into those offering plates.

Administration Days

Overview: Teenagers will offer their enthusiasm and energy to support the church office staff.

In this idea, as your teenagers serve the church staff, they'll be working to support the entire church!

Talk with your church administrator, secretary, or pastor to see if the students in the church can serve in the church office. After you get approval, organize administration days by assigning teenagers to the groups listed below. Then schedule administration days throughout the year when teenagers have days off school.

• **Assistant secretaries**—Turn these teenagers over to the church secretary or administrative assistant. Tell the teenagers they'll be completing a variety of tasks.

• **Telephone operators**—Have these teenagers take turns answering the church telephone. Give them a short lesson in proper phone etiquette.

• **Sunday prep workers**—Have these teenagers work to prepare the church for weekend worship. They can fold worship bulletins, straighten chairs, arrange the worship area, or prepare communion elements.

• **Gofers**—Teenagers who drive can run errands for the church staff.

Behind-the-Scenes Look

Overview: Teenagers will learn what takes place behind the scenes of the church.

Many teenagers simply don't know what's involved in running a church. They may attend youth group, Sunday school, and worship services, but their understanding ends there. If teenagers really are going to be a part of the church, they have to understand how it works. Here are a few things you can do to teach your teenagers that church is a lot more than hymns on Sunday morning.

• Create an organizational chart similar to the ones businesses use to show how different arms of a company work together. Include paid employees, volunteers, and various committees that together create the functional church.

• Lead teenagers on a tour of the church, including the offices. Explain to teenagers which church activities—especially behind-the-scenes activities—take place in each area.

• Invite various church leaders to talk briefly to the teenagers about what they do.

• Invite teenagers to attend church business meetings. Talk with teenagers about what will be happening at the meetings. Have teenagers discuss the importance of the decisions to be made, and encourage them to pay attention.

• Discuss the meetings the next time you meet. Talk about what happened, who the decisions will affect, and how the decisions will affect those people.

• Have teenagers join the church's various committees. They'll learn a lot about the administration and planning of the church, and they'll be able to report back about decisions that affect the group.

Big Stuff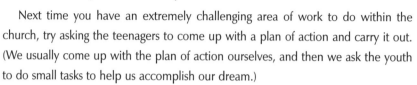

Overview: Youth will plan some big, important stuff in your church.

Next time you have an extremely challenging area of work to do within the church, try asking the teenagers to come up with a plan of action and carry it out. (We usually come up with the plan of action ourselves, and then we ask the youth to do small tasks to help us accomplish our dream.)

Is your children's Sunday school attendance failing? Ask the youth if they have any ideas. This idea was presented to one church, and the youth came up with their own community visitation plan. Adults were needed to help them carry out the plan, but it was their own idea.

One Church's Story

"We asked our youth to help plan the new building for our church. They told us it was very important to have a gymnasium large enough for a full-size basketball court. Unfortunately, the church hadn't put enough money in the budget. So the teenagers contributed the money themselves!"

Does your church have a yearly church leadership retreat? Some churches have these events for their committee leaders. To add some spark to the next one, have the pastor meet with the youth and present the vision for the church and the outcome of the planning retreat. Be sure teenagers understand the importance of the retreat; then let them plan it. Be there to give input, but allow them to pray over it, work together, and praise the Lord for the outcomes. The adults in your church may welcome the change.

Does your church want to get involved with a local service organization? Instead of having church leaders make the connections with the local organization, let the youth do it. That way, instead of the adults making all the arrangements and then asking the teenagers to simply show up and work, the teenagers will have the experience of making the initial contact. Also, let the teenagers recruit volunteers for the work.

Approaching this kind of ministry with teenagers can be very exciting. The teenagers will be doing a great deal of work and feeling good about it. However, remember to provide the support and direction they need every step of the way. They may be the ones leading a retreat or giving a presentation, but they'll need you to be there to

- pray with them,
- help them remember details and create "to do" lists,
- encourage them,
- help formulate ideas, and
- keep them grounded in the Word of God.

Church Anniversary Celebration

Overview: Teenagers will take an active part in planning and celebrating a church anniversary or other historical occasion.

Several months prior to a church anniversary celebration, arrange for some teenagers to represent your church's youth in working with the planning committee in its development of the event. Obtain permission for the youth to take an active part in the celebration by re-enacting some of the early historical stories or events.

Begin by working with the teenagers to develop a historical outline or sketch that details some of the events surrounding the beginning of the church. This can be accomplished by reading through old records, newsletters, and board meeting minutes and by doing interviews with senior church members.

After they have completed an adequate amount of research, work with the teenagers to plan a series of skits about the historical beginning of the church. Arrange for these skits to be used either as promotions leading up to the anniversary celebration or as part of the celebration itself. They can be performed in worship or in conjunction with other church activities.

This activity can also be used for other special events, including building dedications or any other occasions that celebrate the congregation's roots.

Church Brochure

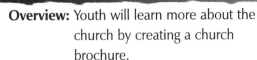

Overview: Youth will learn more about the church by creating a church brochure.

Youth can learn a great deal and provide a service to the church by being the authors, reporters, and editors for a church brochure. This can be done in one of two ways:

• Some churches have not gotten around to creating or updating a brochure. If your church is one of these and if the church members are open-minded, you may be able to convince them to let the youth do it.

• Some churches have professional, up-to-date brochures already finished and in use. If your church is one of these, there still may be a need for a brochure that explains your church's programs to teenagers or children. See if your group can create its own style of brochure for a specific audience.

After you've decided which type of brochure is best for your youth program to create, you can have a lot of fun doing the project. Have your group form teams consisting of one photographer and two writers. Send each team to two or three programs or meetings to gather information about the various church activities.

Make sure your brochure covers all program areas within the church. Consider Sunday school, adult education, evangelism, women's ministry, men's ministry, youth ministry, trustees, custodians, deacons, administration, child care, senior citizens, missions, and counseling. Don't forget to include outreach events. The pastors and other church leaders also may have some ideas and pointers to consider.

After teenagers collect their information, put the brochure together. This is a project that will use many talents. Some of your youth can work on layout and design. Find some work for your artists and poets. This project also will educate your teenagers. They'll learn a great deal as they go on their investigative missions.

As your brochure nears completion, be sure to have a professional or a detail-oriented person proofread your work. There probably are people who can edit and proofread within your congregation.

When the project is finished, make sure the brochures get used. Display them around your church building. Send them out with the church newsletter, youth newsletter, or children's quarterly. You may find that they're also welcome at homeless shelters, the local chamber of commerce, and local grocery stores. Equip the church ushers and those who call on first-time visitors with the brochures.

Variations: Have the youth make videotaped commercials about some of your church programs. Show them during the refreshment time on Sunday mornings. Or have the youth update the church bulletin boards. Send them out to photograph and interview a variety of church leaders in action. Their creativity could add real excitement to your church bulletin boards.

Otherwise, it may be time for your church to make a picture directory. Picture directories are done by private companies, but the opening pages are done by local churches and open to creativity. Your group may want to take pictures of church events for the opening pages of this directory.

Comment Cards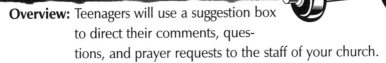

Overview: Teenagers will use a suggestion box to direct their comments, questions, and prayer requests to the staff of your church.

Put a suggestion box in an accessible location in your youth group's meeting room or Sunday school classroom. On the box, put a sign that says, "A direct line to church leaders." Tell your teenagers that they're always welcome to talk with you or other church leaders directly. Explain that the box is meant to make it easier (and less intimidating) for youth to make suggestions, ask questions, or ask for help.

Tell your teenagers that suggestions about the youth group and the administration of the church are especially appropriate. Explain that they'll receive responses if they include their names and telephone numbers or addresses on their suggestions. Assure teenagers that all suggestions will be considered and will be kept confidential (except for cases where someone is in danger).

Keep the box locked, and assure the group that only the church leaders will look at the suggestions. Next to the suggestion box, put a stack of the "Suggestion Forms" found on page 56. Check the box every week, and make sure that someone on the staff addresses each suggestion with an encouraging note, a telephone call, or a face-to-face meeting whenever possible.

Community Connections

Overview: Youth will serve as representatives to other youth programs in the community and will serve on a church program planning committee.

Nearly every community includes a wide variety of youth organizations addressing multiple needs. Youth workers in a community have common interests and often have common goals, but they don't always have a mechanism for sharing with each other. There may be little communication between organizations, and as a result there may be needs of youth that aren't being met.

Your youth can serve a need in the community by joining or starting up a consortium of youth organizations to communicate with each other regarding goals and

Suggestion Form

Name: _____

Telephone: _____

Address: _____

_____

E-mail: _____

Suggestion   Question   Need   Other (Circle One)

_____

_____

_____

_____

I understand that any of the church leaders may address this suggestion, question, or concern, but if possible, I'd like _____ to get back to me.

Suggestion Form

Name: _____

Telephone: _____

Address: _____

_____

E-mail: _____

Suggestion   Question   Need   Other (Circle One)

_____

_____

_____

_____

I understand that any of the church leaders may address this suggestion, question, or concern, but if possible, I'd like _____ to get back to me.

programs. The best way to put together a group like this is to invite all the youth workers in the community to discuss how they can share with each other.

Try including some teenagers in this process by allowing them to serve as representatives of your group. Have these representatives attend meetings to learn about programs of other area youth-serving organizations. After the teenagers have a clear understanding of the goals and programming of each organization, have them report the information back to church leaders, especially those who are involved in planning youth programming.

Consider helping teenage representatives publish a newsletter that highlights all youth activities in the community. Teenagers could write about youth programming in the community, keeping all youth-serving organizations up-to-date with information on activities.

From the Ground Up

Overview: Teenagers will research and propose a new ministry for their church, then take their idea through the proper administrative procedures to determine its viability.

To begin, have youth develop a plan for proposing a new ministry for the church. The plan might include interviewing members about what needs they have, looking at needs in the community, and visiting other churches to look at and evaluate their programs. You may want to set up committees to complete the specific tasks required.

When your group has gathered its data, have group members present to each other all the information they collected and vote on which ministry program would best meet the needs of your church and community.

This may be the time to sit down with your pastor or governing board to see what channels are normally followed when someone presents a new idea. After deciding on a new ministry program, guide the group in taking the necessary steps to see if the project would be viable for your church.

Teenagers may be surprised at the amount of information that still needs to be gathered and presented. Explain that for most programs, some standard considerations might include

- staffing,

- space,

- budget,

- supplies, and

- liability.

For example, let's say your group has decided the church should provide a mid-week club for Christian student-athletes. Have they considered who will staff the program, how much staff will cost, how much equipment will cost, whether you'll need to rent practice and playing fields, whether you'll need to pay officials, and how much insurance is?

Once teenagers have finished collecting all the necessary information, have them go through the necessary process to present their findings to church leadership. Whether or not their idea comes to fruition, group members will in the future be less likely to offhandedly think, "How come we never do...?"

Hot off the Press

Overview: Teenagers will write, design, produce, and distribute the church newsletter.

Ask the person who is responsible for the church newsletter if the youth can serve him or her by creating the church newsletter, either for one issue or on an ongoing basis. Have your group form committees that will handle each of the essential steps in creating, producing, and distributing the newsletter. For example, you may need an organizing committee, an interviewing committee, a writing committee, a designing committee, a copying and folding committee, and a distribution committee.

Have each committee work with the person usually responsible for its phase of the newsletter creation. Encourage that person to assist and supervise the teenagers but to avoid doing the work for them. Challenge teenagers to create a newsletter they can be proud of. Have the organizing committee keep the newsletter moving through the process and check with church leaders at each stage to make sure the newsletter is acceptable and has the appropriate information.

After the newsletter has been written, designed, and printed, have the distribution committee give it to church members in your church's usual way. Make sure the newsletter shows that the youth group designed, created, and produced it.

Matching Grants

Overview: Teenagers will actively support a ministry in your community, and your church will match their financial contributions to the ministry.

They're called "matching grants," and nonprofit organizations *love* them. The idea is for an employee to donate money to a cause; then his or her employer matches the amount. This doubles the donation and encourages employees to look past themselves and support community causes.

Challenge teenagers to identify a ministry in your community and ask the church to provide a matching grant up to a certain amount. Set up two criteria for the ministry selection: The teenagers must be actively involved in the ministry, and the ministry must be consistent with the church's values and mission statement.

Be clear about the criteria; then support whatever ministry your teenagers select. This activity requires your teenagers to evaluate ministries for impact and effectiveness and to make an investment of time and money in the ministry. What your teenagers learn during these ministry experiences will mold them for a lifetime.

Ask your church to approve a maximum matching grant amount. Then set a fund-raising goal with your youth that's equal to that amount. Ask teenagers to brainstorm about ways to meet the goal, such as getting donations or holding a "Servant-for-a-Day" auction. Strive for a variety of activities, not just getting to the total quickly. Publicize the effort churchwide; then set a deadline and get to work.

When you've reached your goal, go as a group to present the final gift to the ministry. Invite the entire church to join you. This will give older members the opportunity to see how involved, caring teenagers can make a difference. And it will let young children see that part of growing into adolescence is serving others.

Mission-Board Minutes

Overview: Youth will work with the missions committee to plan a churchwide missions meeting.

Invite your teenagers to sit in on a missions board meeting to get a feel for how this committee functions in your church. Then encourage youth to work with the missions committee to invite a missionary family to the church for an evening of informative learning and interaction with the entire church body. The youth will need to enlist the help of the missions board to plan and execute this event.

Help teenagers work with the missions committee to plan the type of presentation they'd like the missionaries to share with the church (videos, slides, hands-on activities, a speech), the refreshments, and related programming (music, offering, children's activities). The entire missions night should be sponsored by the youth with the help of the missions board.

Teenagers can issue an invitation to the missionaries, announce the event during a worship service, plan and oversee the activities, assign workers, follow up before the event to remind volunteers what each is expected to bring, officiate during the missions night, and organize cleanup.

Once the missions night is over, youth should attend a follow-up missions board meeting to discuss the event and any improvements to make in the future. Then help teenagers write thank you notes to the missionaries and the missions board members who assisted them.

People Spotlight

Overview: Students will organize and maintain a "People Spotlight" bulletin board.

As teenagers work together to create a bulletin board spotlighting special people, they'll help people in your church get to know each other. They'll also make some new friends!

Ask your church leaders for permission to place a bulletin board in a heavily traveled area of your church. Once you've got permission, organize your teenagers in the following teams.

• **Photographers**—These people are responsible for making arrangements to photograph people "in the spotlight."

• **Interviewers**—These students are responsible for interviewing the people who are in the spotlight. Photocopy the "Spotlight" questionnaire (p. 62), and give the copies to your interviewers.

• **Decorators**—These students will place the photos and the interviews on the bulletin board in a visually appealing way.

Ask teenagers to pick five people from the church they'd like to interview and place "in the spotlight" for the rest of the church to see. Once they've chosen their five people, ask volunteers to call the people and tell them what you're planning. Instruct the interviewers and photographers to schedule times to interview and photograph their subjects.

Once your spotlighted people have been interviewed and photographed, schedule a time for the group to get together and discuss the material they have. Give the photos and interviews to the decorators. Make sure these people have the supplies they need to make the bulletin board look fantastic.

Encourage teenagers to make this an ongoing effort, interviewing and photographing new people every few weeks. Plan to change the bulletin board every month or so.

Recruitment Lunch

Overview: Teenagers will host a lunch to help recruit volunteers to teach Sunday school.

The next time your church is searching for volunteer Sunday school teachers, have the teenagers get involved. Help the teenagers host a recruitment lunch so the recruitment team can let people know what the church needs.

First, ask the person in charge of "hiring" Sunday school teachers to visit the youth group or youth Sunday school class. He or she can talk to the teenagers about what positions need to be filled and what kind of people they're looking for. Encourage teenagers to ask questions and take notes.

Then have the teenagers announce in church—and in bulletins, newsletters, and Web pages—that everyone is welcome to join them for lunch to learn more about the volunteer needs for Sunday school.

Plan the lunch for after church. You can make it as elaborate and decorative or as simple as you want. At the least, have a few teenagers speak to everyone about the impact volunteer Sunday school teachers have made in their lives. Then the teenagers can introduce the person in charge of recruiting volunteers. He or she can speak for a few minutes about the positions, what the church is looking for in volunteers, what volunteers can expect, and what the church expects from volunteers. Afterward, as people eat, set out sign-up sheets at a table so potential recruits can write their names, phone numbers, and positions of interest.

Research Assistants

Overview: Teenagers will provide illustrations, video, multimedia, or other resources for the pastor's sermon.

After clearing the idea with the senior pastor of your church, ask for youth

Spotlight

- Tell us about your childhood.

- Name five of the best books you've read.

- How did you become a Christian?

- What do you like best about our church?

- What public or church groups are you most active in?

- What's your favorite Scripture passage? Why?

volunteers who will help research an upcoming sermon for your pastor. Have the volunteers talk with the senior pastor to find out the topic, Scripture text, and type of information that's needed.

After your volunteers have the basic information, direct them to the resources you and the church have. Encourage volunteers to search for stories, object lessons, and teaching ideas. You also can direct teenagers to commentaries and Bible dictionaries for interesting and important insights. After the volunteers have looked through the church's resources, brainstorm with them about other ideas, such as relevant movie clips, comic strips, music, or resources from the Internet. Make sure teenagers write down all the ideas they come up with.

Before the volunteers present their resource ideas to the senior pastor, have them each spend at least fifteen minutes reflecting on the Scripture text the pastor plans to use. Encourage teenagers to use the resources they've found if those resources help their personal study.

Then have the volunteers share with the pastor the insights they had during their personal reflection *and* the list of resources they compiled. Encourage your pastor to use as many of the ideas as possible during the sermon. And inform the teenagers that time constraints limit the number of ideas the pastor can use. Make sure the teenagers get credit for their work through a note in the bulletin or a word of thanks from the pastor during the sermon.

Training Committee Chairs

Overview: Youth will become involved in church committees after the committee chairs have been trained on involving youth.

Teenagers often are willing to be part of a regular or special committee at the church, but they may lose interest because they aren't actively involved in the program. Adults are often the culprits just because they don't know how to actively involve the youth.

Teenagers have less history on a project or an issue in the church, and often they can simplify a situation for everyone involved. Youth also have many leadership skills to offer.

Before making an effort to involve youth, a church should define the roles youth will play on committees and decide the level of involvement the church is committed to allowing. Placing youth on committees without making these decisions first may lead to discouragement.

Train the adults who chair the committees in the church—and possibly other adult committee members—on how to work with and involve youth on committees. Include training topics like these:

• **Age characteristics and abilities of youth**—This can include topics such as peer pressure, shyness speaking around adults, the need to draw information out of them, and the differences between a twelve-year-old and a seventeen-year-old.

• **Role of youth on committees**—Youth need to do more than sit on a committee. They need to feel that their ideas are of value. They also need to take an active leadership role at times. They can be given a job and be expected to complete it.

• **Ways to include youth on committees**—They can contribute ideas, serve on planning committees, set up rooms for meetings, or call other people to ask them to volunteer.

• **Leadership possibilities for youth on committees and at events**—Possibilities include leading prayer, leading songs, or leading activities.

• **Writing volunteer job descriptions for youth on committees**—It's important to consider their individual gifts, interests, and time constraints.

• **Recognizing youth for their contributions**—Teenagers, like adults, appreciate being recognized for their work.

Provide this training in an evening or half-day session. The main value of the training comes in helping adults understand how to look at youth in a different way and how they can help teenagers feel welcome and valued. Young people have many special skills and insights to provide to ongoing or special church committees. The key is to unlock these treasures by training the adults.

VBS Evaluation

Overview: Teenagers will evaluate advertisements for various VBS programs.

To help your church choose a vacation Bible school program, have your teenagers evaluate VBS advertisements. Ask your church's education director and Sunday school teachers for any VBS advertisements or direct-mail pieces they have. Bring them and any current Christian education magazines available to your meeting.

Tell your teenagers they're going to create a comparison chart of the VBS programs available. The chart should include the name, publisher, theme (such as "circus" or "space"), biblical content theme (such as "Jesus' life" or "God's love"), cost, and components. The cost and components sections should be detailed, as well as the extra costs for each component—"$20 for each student book" or "$7 for a set of twelve craft items," for example.

Have students form pairs, and distribute paper and pens to each pair. Then have everyone search through the advertisements and other materials to create separate charts. When teenagers have looked through all the materials, have them combine what they learned into one chart to present to the VBS selection team.

Web Page Proposals

Overview: Teenagers will design a Web page for the church.

This activity is somewhat risky because you can't predict the outcome. That's also the reason this activity can be so powerful.

Here's the challenge for your teenagers: Design a Web page for your church. But do more than just design an attractive, interactive page to draw people to church services. Rather, communicate what your church is doing, and explain how those activities meet the criteria of what Jesus expects his church to be.

This raises some questions for teenagers to sort through:

• What *is* a church supposed to be? to do? to believe?

Have teenagers read 1 Corinthians 12 together and outline what they think it says about being the church.

• What does *your* church believe? What does your church do?

• What sets your congregation apart from the dozens of other churches in your area?

• What does your church offer? require? demand?

Ask your teenagers to surf the Internet a bit and download Web pages of other congregations. Help them sort through what they can learn about those churches from their Web pages. What are the purposes of the pages?

As your teenagers sketch designs for a Web page for *your* church, they'll be growing in their understanding of what it means to be the church in the world, to represent Christ, and to proclaim the Gospel.

You may discover that your teenagers have a low regard for some aspect of your church programming. If that's the case, invite a staff member of your church to discuss the teenagers' concerns. Help your teenagers see how they fit into the church. See if areas of weakness they discover can be addressed and filled by teenagers.

Show the proposed designs to your church staff, and have the group decide if one or more of the ideas can be used to create an actual Web site. If so, ask selected members of your group to handle the administration of the site.

Note: Resources for Web page design change as quickly as the Web changes. Call local Internet providers for information concerning simple and free design software you can download, and give your teenagers a shot at doing design on screen.

Youth Concerns Committee

Overview: Generations will work together to help coordinate effective church programming.

The purpose of this committee is to give youth the opportunity to be a part of church programming. The youth concerns committee would consist of any students who are interested in being involved in the formation of church programming. This committee would meet monthly with church leadership and would be granted opportunities to give feedback and suggestions regarding the various ministries in the church and their effects on the youth.

This committee would need an adult coach well-versed in the formation and implementation of church programming. This coach would help lead the youth concerns committee in forming proposals and articulating any youth concerns to be addressed in the monthly meeting with the church leadership. The coach's main role is to provide support and direction, not run the meeting. When the meeting or student follow-through seems to be struggling, the coach can provide guidance to empower the youth to take ownership in the committee and in the church.

Youth Evangelism Subcommittee

Overview: Teenagers will form a subcommittee of the church outreach committee and develop a plan for telling other teenagers about Christ.

If your church doesn't already have teenagers on the church outreach committee, help youth develop a plan to be included as representatives or members.

As a part of the outreach committee, request permission to form a subcommittee of youth and adults who will address specific issues involving youth evangelism. The specific purpose of this subcommittee is to develop a plan for telling other teenagers about Christ and bringing them into the church family. Ideas for this sub-committee to consider might include hosting a special youth-oriented concert or an after-game pizza party or developing a teen-friendly brochure about the church.

Have the committee spend some time discussing what obstacles are present in the church and youth ministry that might keep some skeptical teenagers from wanting to become active participants. Start by discussing the following:

• What activities and programs does our church offer that are especially attractive to teenagers?

• Name activities or programs teenagers might not feel welcome to participate in.

• List our youth events and activities that have been especially meaningful to teenagers.

• What are some things our group might do that would keep other teenagers from wanting to participate in it?

• List some things we can do to make our church more attractive to teenagers.

• Name some things we can do to make our youth ministry more attractive to other teenagers.

Family Events

Adult Scavenger Hunt

Overview: Teenagers will search the community for various types of adults.

Next time you want to plan a scavenger hunt for your youth program, try hunting for adults instead of thimbles and kite string! Although teenagers aren't instructed to make this a *family* event, it will become one without even trying.

Recruit responsible adult drivers; then have teenagers form teams of three to five, depending on vehicle space. Each vehicle should have room for at least one additional person. Give each carload a photocopy of the "Adult Scavenger Hunt" list on page 70. Give teams a time limit, and send them out to collect adults.

As teams collect "cargo," they may drop the person(s) off at the church and go back out into the community to keep looking until time is up. Be ready to make the "collected" people feel comfortable. Many of them will be the parents or grandparents of your students. Others will be family friends.

Have refreshments ready to serve. You also may want to have some board games or puzzles set out to keep people feeling comfortable and to encourage them to socialize until all the cars and cargo are back.

When everyone has returned, give out small prizes to teams for accomplishments like collecting the most adults, bringing an adult from the farthest location, and finding adults with the widest variety in ages. Be sure to also thank the adults who were willing to come on such short notice. Then give a short devotion, and allow people to socialize before they're driven home. Introduce everyone at some point during the event.

Blended Families

Overview: Teenagers will initiate a program that helps families of your church get to know each other better.

Have teenagers invite everyone in your church to sign up for a family meals program to help families get to know one another over a meal. You may want to have families commit to the program for an entire quarter. During sign up, have families indicate whether they'd be willing to host a meal for two other families. If not, they can just sign up to be guests. After families have had a chance to sign up, coordinate the dinners by putting the families in groups of three. Form a group of two or four families if necessary.

Post a list in your church that displays where families will be eating, the telephone numbers of each family involved, and three "ice-breaking" questions to discuss at the meals, such as "What's the most beautiful place you've ever been?" Either designate an evening during the next two weeks as the official family meals night, or simply have families work out the schedule themselves.

Encourage families to include their teenagers and children in the meals so various generations in the church have an opportunity to connect with each other. Make sure the family meals are available to single adults and single parents by encouraging them to sign up.

Every two weeks, post a new list with different groups of three families. Then remind the families to get together for a meal sometime during those next two weeks. Check in with the families from time to time to see how the program is going. Challenge families to take the relationships beyond meals to form mentoring relationships, prayer partners, and family friends. Allow an opportunity for new people to enter (and others to leave) the program every quarter.

Adult Scavenger Hunt

Find adults who fit into the following categories, and bring them with you. Come back to the church when you need to drop off your cargo.

Be sure to tell the people you take as cargo that they won't be returned home for an hour or more. They can drive their own cars if they must leave earlier.

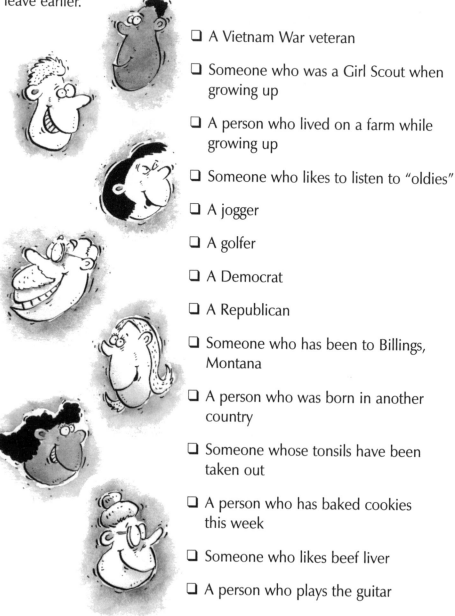

- ❏ A Vietnam War veteran
- ❏ Someone who was a Girl Scout when growing up
- ❏ A person who lived on a farm while growing up
- ❏ Someone who likes to listen to "oldies"
- ❏ A jogger
- ❏ A golfer
- ❏ A Democrat
- ❏ A Republican
- ❏ Someone who has been to Billings, Montana
- ❏ A person who was born in another country
- ❏ Someone whose tonsils have been taken out
- ❏ A person who has baked cookies this week
- ❏ Someone who likes beef liver
- ❏ A person who plays the guitar

Building Families With Photographs

Overview: Youth will organize family activities and document them with photographs.

Photography can be a valuable skill for youth to develop, and it also can be a positive family-building tool. This idea combines photography with planning and providing family-building experiences.

If you have an accomplished amateur or professional photographer in the church, ask him or her to lead some courses on photography. If not, you might contact a local newspaper or professional photography studio to find someone to volunteer for the position.

Plan and promote this idea as an educational program on photography for families. Offer at least six meetings. The first three or four sessions should concentrate on the basics of photography and on techniques for capturing family experiences. Training should include technical aspects of photography as well as how to capture emotion, activity, and special memories on film.

For the last two or three sessions, have families go out together on outings such as picnics, hikes, recreation, arts, or any other activities that involve interaction among family members. In addition to having fun as families, the goal will be to capture the activities in photographs.

Have families review photos from the last activity as an introduction to the next one. The leader of the program should do some light critiquing or lead a discussion about the characteristics of photos, but the primary purpose will be to learn some skills while having family fun.

At the conclusion of the program, have each family prepare a collection of photographs from the activities for display at the church. Photo memories, especially those that show family members enjoying each other, help build a sense of family and community. These memories also can be organized into photo albums for families to take home.

Conflict-Resolution Class

Overview: Teenagers will initiate a family conflict-resolution class.

In this activity, teenagers will research, develop, promote, and facilitate a family conflict-resolution class. This idea probably will work best as a Saturday workshop.

First, youth will have to decide who the target audience will be. While your group may want to open the class to all families, it may be best to limit this class to what your group knows best: families with teenagers. Of course, if your church is large and has adequate staff, a broader spectrum may be appropriate.

Next, have your group decide what issues they'd like to cover in the class. Teenagers will likely draw from their own experiences in family conflict. They may want to address issues such as curfew, finances, dating, and discipline.

Encourage teenagers to focus not only on problems they think should be included in the program, but also on possible solutions. Make sure topics such as communication skills, appropriate limits, and anger control are included.

At this point, your group should decide who will facilitate the workshop. Perhaps the youth leader would be the perfect person to lead the class. Or if finances allow, perhaps your church would want to hire an outside speaker or counselor. Either way, make sure your teenagers stay involved in deciding what the agenda will be. They also can participate in facilitating discussion.

> **Tip**
>
> *If serious conflicts come up during this meeting, you may want to encourage participants to use the conflict-resolution skills your group has researched to resolve them. Or you may want to suggest that people deal with these conflicts now or later, outside the class.*

If students want to lead the workshop themselves, make sure you've incorporated plenty of development time before your event. Have group members form pairs or trios to research specific topics they want to cover. To research their topics, encourage teenagers to get books from the library and interview counselors. Then have them develop a time table for the event and discuss how each topic will be presented. Help teenagers practice conflict-resolution skills before the workshop.

Finally, make sure teenagers advertise and invite families to their event! At the workshop, encourage plenty of discussion between parents and kids about specific topics.

Dumb-Game Olympics

Overview: Teenagers will spend time in fun and zany fellowship with other generations.

The dumb-game olympics can be an annual event that brings every generation together in your church or community. The purpose of this event is to allow people who normally might not interact with one another the opportunity to interact in a fun and safe way. This also is a good event to encourage families to bring friends and neighbors to.

The event itself is exactly what it sounds like: a team competition in a bunch of silly events. These events are specifically designed to even out the playing field so everyone who participates has an equal opportunity to succeed. Also, these events allow individuals to laugh and enjoy one another's company in an intergenerational setting. You'll want to present the winning team with a small, cheap trophy item (such as a painted rock or a plastic crown) that can be passed on from year to year.

Have participants form four to five equal teams. There should be both males and females and a wide variety of ages on the teams. Encourage family members to be on the same team. It's important to make it clear that not everyone has to participate in every event. In some instances, individuals may wish to not participate in any events. Respect their choices, and encourage them to participate in other ways, such as acting as judges.

One Church's Story

"When our church hosted the dumb-game olympics, the event was a huge success. This activity provided a natural opportunity for families to get to know one another. It also helped kids and their parents enjoy playing with each other—something many of them hadn't done in a while.

"This event also served to bring some new families to the church. Their teenagers had been attending youth functions, but after the dumb-game olympics, the entire family started going to church!"

Set up a series of simple games from resources such as Group's *On-the-Edge Games for Youth Ministry*, *All-Star Games From All-Star Youth Leaders*, and *Building Community in Youth Groups*. Plan to fill an hour to an hour and a half with games that are fun, funny, fair, and inclusive to age and gender. You'll want to pick a few silly relays, some messy games, and some loud and obnoxious games.

Award points to the team that wins each game, but don't stop there. Give out points when teams cheer for one another, are very loud, come up with songs and cheers for their teams, and even bribe the judges with gifts and admiration. There should be no real winners or losers at the end of the day—just happy players.

When the olympics are over, present the trophy to the team with the most points and a charge to guard the trophy at all costs so it can be re-presented at next year's event. You may want to complete the afternoon with a potluck dinner.

Family Choir

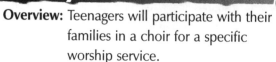

Overview: Teenagers will participate with their families in a choir for a specific worship service.

Encourage youth to become involved in your church's music program by working with your pastor and worship leader to designate a special day for a family choir. This choir can be as spontaneous or rehearsed as you would like it to be.

If your music director is willing, ask him or her to select music that appeals to your youth group. Offer suggestions as appropriate. Ask the music director to plan at least one rehearsal the week before the family choir is scheduled to sing. Instead of seating the choir by parts, allow families to stand in clusters. This is a great, low-commitment way to help youth explore the opportunities available to them through the church's music program.

Family Crossword Swap

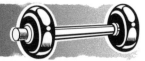

Overview: Youth will work with their families to create crossword puzzles and then solve other families' crossword puzzles.

Encourage the families in your church to talk together about spiritual values in a fun, relaxing environment. Invite all family members to attend a family crossword swap, and hold the swap after church.

Set up chairs so family members can sit together, and provide tables or clipboards to make writing easier. Also provide some snacks or simple meal items if you're holding the event right after church.

As people arrive, have families sit together, then distribute paper and pens. Ask each family member to talk for a minute about three things he or she learned in Sunday school and church that day. After a few minutes of discussion, explain that each family should create a crossword puzzle about what everyone in the family learned. For example, if Tabitha learned that David was a king, she could contribute the crossword clue "King whose name begins with a 'd.' " Then if Lucas learned that David hid from Saul, he could contribute the crossword clue "King that David hid from." The two clues could intersect each other at the letter "a."

Give families about ten minutes to create their crossword puzzles. Then have families swap crossword puzzles with other families and see if they can fill in the answers.

Family Heritage Festival

Overview: Families will share their heritage with the larger church family.

This activity works if your church is composed primarily of families from the same ethnic background, but a church that's ethnically diverse will have an even *better* time! Depending on the number of teenagers in your church, invite just their families or invite the entire church.

Request that families gather together for a family heritage festival where they will share some aspect of their heritage. Emphasize that a family's heritage may be something other than ethnicity, such as farm or city background. Many families incorporate several heritages, so ask them to select just one to present. For instance, if a family has both a German and an Irish background, they could elect to dress in a traditional German fashion or to bring an Irish dish to share at the potluck. Or if a family is from a farming background, the family might bring vegetables from their garden.

The goal of a family heritage festival isn't to emphasize what separates families in the church from each other. Rather, it's to point out our unity in faith—which is more important than our individual histories. There's a sense of identity that comes with heritage, and celebrating our diversity also can be a celebration of God's power to overcome barriers.

Ask your teenagers to discuss their heritage with their parents. Ask each family to create a simple table-top display about their heritage if they have items that reflect it.

Select a date for a family heritage festival, and organize a potluck featuring heritage-oriented foods. Ask each family to bring a contribution for the potluck and identify the dish on an index card explaining the origins of the food. After the meal, ask each family in attendance to spend three minutes explaining its table-top display, traditional dress, or other indication of heritage.

Challenge your teenagers to present a devotion about unity in Christ. Galatians 3:26-29 and 1 Corinthians 12 are good sources of devotional material. Close with the devotion and a prayer, thanking God for being Lord of all nations.

Family Memories Night

Overview: Students will organize an evening for families to talk about their family history.

Help your congregation honor its families by hosting a family memories night. Organize the event by having teenagers form the following groups.

• **Organizers**—Have these teenagers plan and oversee the entire event. When the event has been planned, these students can serve as encouragers for the other teams during the event.

• **Food**—Give these students the job of organizing the food. A potluck meal works best for this type of event.

• **Publicity**—These students are responsible for letting people know when and where you're having the event. Have these students advertise that you're asking families to come for an evening of dinner and sharing memories. Ask families to bring photographs or souvenirs of major family events.

• **Program**—These students are responsible for ensuring that the program for the evening goes smoothly. Give these students the sample schedule for the evening (see below), and allow them to change it as needed.

Have teenagers get together for an initial planning meeting a few months before this event is to take place. Then allow teenagers to work in their groups over the next few months. Schedule check-up meetings every few weeks.

On the evening of the event, you may want to use the following sample schedule:

6:00 Families arrive and place their memorabilia on a designated wall or table.

6:15 Dinner begins.

6:45 Allow families time to wander around and observe the memorabilia.

7:00 Encourage families to share their memories, both positive and negative.

7:45 Have your pastor or someone else in your congregation offer a short talk about the importance of creating memories with your family.

8:00 Event is over.

Family Pride

Overview: Families will create symbols to demonstrate who they are.

During a Sunday service or midweek meeting, have all the members of your church (including children) gather in the sanctuary or a large fellowship hall. Explain that families are going to work together to create one of three different types of symbols to represent themselves—a family crest, a family collage, or a family sculpture. (If you'd rather not provide all the supplies for all three symbols, simply choose one type of symbol for all the families to do.) Make sure single adults don't do this activity alone. Have them partner with other single friends, be adopted into families for the event, or create their own symbols at a table with other families.

On a few tables in the middle of the room, set out supplies for three different types of symbols. For example, you could set out poster board, markers, rulers, and pencils for the family crests; poster board, markers, magazines, scissors, and glue for the family collages; and self-hardening clay or papier-mâché, water, and wire for the sculptures.

Have family members work together to create a symbol that represents who the family is. You may want to help families get started by providing questions like these:

- What is the one emotion that best describes your family?

- What is your family doing when it's at its very best?

- How does God use your family in the lives of others?

Have families put their last names on their symbols. When families finish their symbols, have a representative from each family describe the symbol to the rest of the church. Post and place the symbols around your church for others to look at over the next few weeks.

Family Progressive Dinner

Overview: Families will host other families for a single course of a full meal and will share family traditions with their guests.

Help your youth work together with their families to create a unique opportunity for sharing special traditions with other families in the church. This is an especially fun activity near Christmastime.

Get a commitment from families two to four weeks in advance. Form groups of six families to keep the size of the progressive dinner manageable. Assign each family in each group one of the following courses: appetizers, soup, salad, vegetables, main course, and dessert.

Encourage your youth to work with their families to select a food item and a family tradition they'd like to share with their dinner guests. Let their creativity take the program planning from there.

> **Tip**
>
> *If your youth are from spread-out areas of the community, you might choose to form groups based on geography. Offer the option of allowing those who live farthest away to bring dinner into the church and set up in various rooms.*

At one of your regular meetings the week before the event, have each teenager draw a map to his or her home. Make five photocopies of each map. Then create an itinerary for each group of six families based on which families are making which portions of the meal. For example, if the Joneses are providing appetizers, they'll be the first house in their group. If the Krafts are providing dessert, they'll be last.

The day of the event, have everyone meet at the church. Distribute each group's itinerary and maps. The family groups will then caravan from house to house, partaking of their meals. Set a time for the families to return to the church after dinner for a time of singing together.

Family Retreat

Overview: Teenagers will plan and help lead a day-long family retreat.

Help youth develop a proposal to obtain permission from church leadership to plan and help lead a family retreat. At least four months before the actual retreat date, meet as a group to begin planning. At the first meeting, provide participants with photocopies of the "Family Retreat Planning Sheet" (p. 79) and the "Planning Time Line" handout (p. 81).

Discuss Part 1 of the "Family Retreat Planning Sheet" as a group. Then have teenagers form the committees listed on Part 2 of the handout for discussion and planning. Each committee should select a leader and a recorder.

Be sure to stress the importance of continued communication and cooperation among the various youth planning committees. This will probably require several planning meetings on a regular basis. The committees themselves also will need to meet several times as they plan their parts of the retreat. Encourage youth to follow their "Planning Time Line" handouts as they plan.

> **Tip**
>
> For a fun family retreat that will appeal to all ages, check out Group Publishing's vacation Bible school resources. With some adaptation, the VBS program could take care of your programming needs.

Suggest that each committee seek adults as members and advisors. This will not only provide each youth committee with additional resources, but it will also help promote the family retreat and gain support from others within the church. Encourage the teenagers to do the planning groundwork themselves, though.

Activities for the retreat might include speakers; team-building activities; games; a family picnic-style meal; an issues forum; drama; role-playing; and craft activities, such as developing a family tree. Or you might schedule some of the other family events described in this book.

Family Retreat Planning Sheet
Part 1

Goal Statement: (What exactly do you want to accomplish during this retreat?)

Theme: (What theme or main idea will you use to help accomplish your goal?)

Location and Date: (Where will the event be held? What will be the retreat date and hours?)

Leaders: (Who will be the leaders? What will their responsibilities be? Will there be a keynote speaker? If so, who will it be?)

....

Part 2

Publicity Committee: How will you get the word out about the retreat? Will forms be available for preregistration? Who will be responsible for inviting leaders and speakers? Who will make reservations at the retreat site and be in communication with the people there?

Finance Committee: What will the budget for this event look like? What will be the approximate costs of the retreat? Will the keynote speaker be paid? Where will the needed money come from? Will there be a charge for families to attend? What steps will have to be taken to seek the necessary finances?

Child Care Committee—Is child care or baby-sitting needed? Who will provide it? If young children are included in the retreat itself, will there be special games, snacks, or additional assistance needed? If so, what will they be? Who will be responsible for them?

Setup/Cleanup Committee—Who will be responsible for setting up the retreat? Who will be responsible for cleaning up afterwards? Who will gather the necessary supplies for the various activities?

Food Committee—Will meals and snacks be served? What will the menu be? Who will prepare and serve the meals? What will they cost?

Activity/Agenda Committee—What will the retreat schedule look like? Which activities will families participate in together? Will there be age-specific activities where adults are together, teenagers are together, and children are together?

Follow-up Committee—Who will be responsible for regularly communicating with the various committee leaders to make sure they're accomplishing their assigned tasks? Who will keep the youth pastor, church board, and senior pastor updated about developing plans?

Planning Time Line

Four months before the event

- Schedule an initial planning meeting. All participants should receive copies of the handouts and be assigned to a committee.
- Individual committees meet to begin planning.
- Choose a location for the retreat and make reservations.
- If you are seeking financial help from the church, the finance committee should meet with the church board or the officer responsible for church financing to discuss possible needs.

Three months before the event

- Whole group meets to hear individual committee reports and to provide suggestions and feedback.
- Individual committees meet again to consider recommendations from the whole group and to continue planning.
- Publicity committee begins initial publicity so participants can put the retreat on their calendars.
- The appropriate person should contact speakers and leaders, including child-care providers (if necessary).
- Finance committee should set a preliminary budget and present it to the church leadership (if necessary).

Two months before the event

- Committees report to the whole group. All plans should be nearly final at this point, including menus, individual assignments, criteria for child care, and the retreat agenda.
- Publicity committee begins publicity blitz.
- Follow-up committee reviews each committee's plan and offers assistance where necessary.

One month before the event

- Publicity committee continues publicity and begins preregistration.
- Whole group meets again for last-minute review and details.
- Everyone gathers equipment and supplies.

One week before the event

- Food committee purchases food for meals and snacks.
- Follow-up committee contacts each committee leader to make sure all details are in place.
- Setup/cleanup committee sets up and decorates retreat location.
- Whole group meets for final briefing and prayer.

One week after the event

- Whole group meets to discuss the retreat planning and outcome.

Family Summit

Overview: Parents and teenagers will share youth group planning ideas and goals.

Give your parents and youth the chance to share their hopes, ideas, and expectations for a predetermined time frame, such as a quarter, a school year, or a calendar year. Establish ahead of time whether this summit will result in a calendar of events or simply generate a pool of ideas to build on.

Give this summit a mountain-climbing theme. Decorate with climbing gear, and place bowls of trail mix around the room to snack on. Before the summit, post newsprint around your meeting room, labeled with the following headings: "Places to Go," "Things to Do," "Topics to Study," "Relationship Goals," "Service Goals," and "Spiritual Growth Goals." Place a red marker and a blue marker near each piece of newsprint.

For the first twenty to thirty minutes, ask parents and youth to write their ideas on the newsprint. Designate red markers for youth comments and blue markers for parent comments. When time is up, collect the newsprint so you can discuss one topic at a time. Look for patterns among the ideas, and note diversity where appropriate. This experience can be valuable in helping your youth group and their parents discover some of the demands you try to meet on a regular basis.

Match the ideas with dates if you've decided to try to do concrete planning. Use this opportunity to recruit parent participation in their areas of interest.

Finish the summit with an outdoor barbecue in celebration of your group's hard work.

Grand-Slam Sleepovers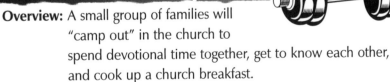

Overview: A small group of families will "camp out" in the church to spend devotional time together, get to know each other, and cook up a church breakfast.

This event can be a great fund-raiser, but its merits really lie in bringing teenagers and families together in a nontraditional way. This also is an event that will help some of the youth-affiliated families get to know the rest of the church as they cook and serve them breakfast.

Invite two to ten families (depending on the size of breakfast you desire) to camp out at the church on a Saturday night. Give these people at least a month's notice so they can be completely free to stay at the church from about 5 p.m. until whenever your church services end the next day. The families should be encouraged to bring all their children if possible. Even Grandma and Grandpa could add a great deal to the evening. The families should bring sleeping bags, toiletries, cooking clothes, and clothes for church on Sunday morning.

The activities for their night together will include the following:

• Participate in a devotional time. You can supply them with one of your favorite devotionals for families with teenagers. Ask one of the teenagers to lead the devotional time.

• Enjoy some get-acquainted activities or games.

• Enjoy a light dinner or snack that a volunteer provides for them.

• Decide on a menu for breakfast the following morning. They may want to make an elaborate breakfast, or they may want to make it simple. It's their choice.

• Shop, prepare, and serve the breakfast for the entire church.

Although shopping at the last minute isn't economical, it can be a fun activity that will help the families to get to know one another. Make sure you have a church check, a credit card, or an envelope of cash on hand. Give the group a number of people to expect at breakfast in the morning.

The families can decide how to divide up the shopping, cooking, and serving chores. Be sure to advise them to assign real responsibilities to the teenagers, such as cooking specific dishes or setting up the church for the meal. (If they're simply told to be "helpers," they'll become bored quickly.)

Even though the group will be task-oriented, you may be amazed to hear about the intergenerational sharing that goes on as the individuals get to know each other in this context.

Advertise to the church that they're invited to a church breakfast on Sunday morning before church. If you want this to be a fund-raiser, list the price.

You may want to have the rest of the youth on hand to clean up after the breakfast on Sunday morning. Your "family group" will be a little tired.

You may want to hold this event the first weekend of each month for several months. That way, the church will get used to the event, and many families will be included.

Holiday Memory Sharing

Overview: Teenagers and their families will share special memories as part of a special holiday celebration.

As part of any holiday celebration, plan an event for families to come together to share special holiday memories. This can be done as a separate event or as part of another event. As a Christmas celebration, it might be included as part of a church decorating party or a special pre-Christmas worship service. Prior to the event, arrange for families to bring refreshments. Ask for one or more families to volunteer as a group to help serve and clean up.

Begin this event by having families meet in the worship area. Lead them in singing or listening to some holiday music. The music accompaniment can be done very simply with either guitar or keyboard, or you can use recorded music. After singing together, have families take turns sharing special family memories of the holiday. If time allows, end with more singing.

> ### Tip
>
> *Encourage families to invite singles or elderly couples who might not be inclined to come to an event like this. Those without extended families can become special adopted family members for the event. Be sure you encourage singles and elderly participants to share their memories as well.*

Life Sports Small Groups

Overview: Families will learn life sports together in a small-group setting that includes a Bible study.

Families need activities they can do together. Team sports are a common priority as children go through school, often at the expense of family time. Many team sports help build good skills, but they aren't necessarily lifetime skills. Some sports, such as tennis, hiking, and cross-country skiing, can be done together as a family for a lifetime.

Sometimes families don't know how to get started playing life sports together. This is where the church comes in. To get a group started, the church coordinator can try to recruit a family to lead the group and then publicize the program based on the leaders' time schedule. Or the coordinator can do a survey of the congregation to find out what life sports the families in the church would be interested in and then follow it up by finding a lead family from those who show interest.

The investment by the church youth worker or small group coordinator is minimal because the program is run by the families themselves. The families will have to invest in recreational equipment, but they may already have some of the equipment.

The basic small-group format is to hold six weekly meetings of a specified length, generally one to one and a half hours. Each meeting consists of four parts: an introduction, a Bible study that relates to the activity, the activity itself, and a sharing of concerns and a time for prayer at the end. One person could serve as the role of Bible discussion leader and another as the activity leader, which may or may not include instruction. This is an excellent opportunity for an adult to co-lead the group with a teenager who has excellent sports skills and can learn how to teach or lead activities.

Hiking as a life sport could include identification of hiking trails in the area, putting together a plan of where to hike at each meeting, and then hiking on five different trails at the next five meetings.

Golf could include basic practice sessions on putting and the short game, driving, and using irons. Then the families would play golf together during the rest of their meetings.

Cross-country skiing would require identification of skill levels and basic instruction if needed. Then, as with hiking, groups could identify ski trails to practice on during the following sessions.

Tennis would again require identification of skill levels and possibly basic instruction, and then the families would gather to play games during their small-group meetings.

Missions Mindset

Overview: Teenagers will talk with their family members about supporting different missions organizations.

A great way for families to foster a sense of togetherness and involvement is to share a common goal. With this idea, families will learn that they can work together to serve others.

Ask your teenagers each to do a little research about one nonprofit organization. Be sure teenagers tell you which organizations they're researching to prevent overlap. Suggest that they look in the local phone book; surf the Internet; find articles in Christian magazines; and talk to church members, church leadership, and denominational offices to find an organization they'd like to know more about. Remind them that there are community organizations and worldwide organizations. (See the list on p. 88 for some suggestions.) Encourage teenagers to learn about the organizations' missions, the different ways people can support the organizations, and how to contact the organizations.

When teenagers have finished their research, invite families to join the teenagers to hear what they've learned. Have each family sit together, and distribute paper and pens. Have each teenager present his or her organization, and encourage families to take notes. After teenagers have finished presenting, ask each family to talk about the type of mission they'd like to support. Ask:

• What kind of involvement is your family looking for—financial or voluntary, for example?

• Which organizations best reflect your entire family's concerns?

• Which organization can best utilize what your family has to offer?

As families talk, remind them that while individuals may seek additional service opportunities, the goal is to find an opportunity everyone in the family feels excited about. Finally, encourage everyone to follow through with what they've decided.

Here are a few national and international organizations families may want to support. Many have local chapters, too. Be sure to check with your denomination for specific missionaries and causes families could support.

American Red Cross
11th Floor
1621 N. Kent St.
Arlington, VA 22209
(703) 248-4222
www.redcross.org

Big Brothers Big Sisters of America
230 N. 13th Street
Philadelphia, PA 19107
(215) 567-7000
www.bbbsa.org

Compassion International
Colorado Springs, CO 80997
(719) 594-9900
www.ci.org

Habitat for Humanity International
121 Habitat St.
Americus, GA 31709
(912) 924-6935
www.habitat.org

Target Earth
3015 P Hopyard Rd.
Pleasanton, CA 94558
(925) 462-2439
www.targetearth.org

World Vision Inc.
P.O. Box 9716
Federal Way, WA 98063-9716
1-888-511-6598
www.worldvision.org

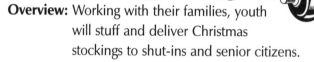

Secret Santa Stockings

Overview: Working with their families, youth will stuff and deliver Christmas stockings to shut-ins and senior citizens.

This event will help youth and their families connect with shut-ins and older members of the congregation. Shhh! Keep your work a secret so the recipients will have a Christmas surprise!

Begin this project several months in advance. Check with the church secretary for a list of the shut-ins and senior members in your congregation. Determine the number of stockings needed (one per person). Stockings may be purchased or created in any of the following ways:

• **Sewn stockings**—Talented youth or adults may sew fabric stockings.

• **Decorated gift bags**—On the front of a solid-color gift bag, draw a stocking, or glue a stocking-shape construction paper cutout.

• **Decorated shoeboxes**—Wrap the bottom and the lid of a shoe box separately in Christmas or solid-color wrapping paper. Glue a stocking-shape construction paper cutout to the lid.

Determine the kinds of stocking stuffers you'll need. Use the list in the margin to get started. Fill in quantities next to the items you want to include.

Check with your missions fund treasurer if you need financial help in acquiring the stockings and stuffers. Or ask for donations from families in the church. Give families photocopies of the list in the margin, and ask them to sign up to bring specified quantities of the items needed. Avoid placing requests in the bulletin or newsletter. Remember, it's a secret!

Choose an evening or afternoon early in December to assemble, fill, and deliver the stockings. Prepare the stockings or materials to make them, and have the stuffers set up an assembly line. Invite youth and their families to work together to create and fill the stockings. Include a Christmas card from the church in each stocking. Play Christmas music to set a holiday mood.

Divide the stockings among the families, and encourage entire families to deliver them. Provide each family with the names, addresses, and telephone numbers of their stockings' recipients. A map or directions from the church to the recipients' homes or apartments may be helpful also.

The smiles and hugs from surprised recipients make the effort of this family event worthwhile!

Stocking Stuffer Ideas

Postage stamps

Letter-size envelopes

Christmas and all-occasion cards

Stationery and writing tablets

Single packets of coffee, tea, cocoa, and cider

Single servings of soup (canned or dried) and crackers

Fresh fruit and nuts

Small loaves of specialty breads

Holiday cookies

Candy canes and peppermints

Pocket-size packets of facial tissues

Summer Movie Night

Overview: Teenagers will plan and host a community family event on the church lawn.

If your church has a video projector, a screen, and a jumbo-size container of bug repellent, you're ready for a family-friendly summer movie night!

For this project you'll need to form three task-forces:

• **Publicity commandos**—The publicity commandos are responsible for getting people to attend. They'll communicate the who, what, when, where, and how of the event. They can distribute flyers in the community, place ads at the playgrounds, or do whatever they think will work best.

• **Logistics commandos**—The logistics commandos will take care of selecting a date, rounding up equipment, and staffing the event. Here's where you'll need the most people helping.

• **Follow-up commandos**—The follow-up commandos make certain every visitor who attends is identified for follow-up.

Start by selecting a date that makes your movie night available for the largest number of people. Since you're after families that include children, consider Friday or Saturday nights when children may be allowed to stay up later. Arrange for your location to be outside on the lawn or in the parking lot. Provide chairs, and keep a door open so restrooms are available. Select a recent video release likely to appeal to children and with a rating that won't create problems.

Use a video projection unit to show the movie. If you have a building with a smooth, white exterior wall, use it as your screen. Otherwise, set up a regular screen outside (try borrowing one if you don't have one—and brace it securely so a gust of wind doesn't send it tumbling), or hang a tightly stretched white sheet. The surface must be reflective. Test your system *before* you schedule the event!

In publicity pieces, inform the community that entire families are invited and that there is absolutely no charge for the movie. In fact, you probably *can't* charge for viewing the movie without breaking copyright laws. Provide popcorn and soda snacks either free or for a very nominal charge.

One way to collect names of participants is to have a door prize and preprinted tickets to win it. On the tickets, ask for names, addresses, and phone numbers. A door prize of a prepaid video rental from an area store is both inexpensive and attractive to families who would attend an event like this. Use the information for follow-up efforts.

Thanks, Mom and Dad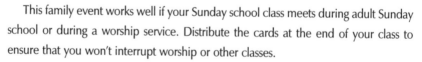

Overview: Teenagers will create thank you cards for their parents.

This family event works well if your Sunday school class meets during adult Sunday school or during a worship service. Distribute the cards at the end of your class to ensure that you won't interrupt worship or other classes.

Gather teenagers together and ask them to share things they appreciate about their parents. As teenagers share, record their answers on a piece of newsprint taped to the wall. When teenagers have shared, distribute sheets of paper and markers. Have teenagers create thank you cards for their parents, using ideas they have or borrowing them from the newsprint.

When teenagers have created their cards, tell them they're going to present their cards to their parents. Tell them they're going to find their parents just after they've finished their Sunday school class or worship. Remind them to be respectful and polite.

As you travel together to find parents, instruct teenagers to make a big deal about their presentations to their parents. Ask them to make sure several people hear what they're saying to their parents as they present their cards to them. Ask them to say something like "Mom and Dad, I'm so glad that God gave you to me to be my parents. Thanks for everything you've done for me."

If you have students whose parents aren't at church, remind those students to present their cards to their parents when they get home.

Ministry Opportunities

Advent Fair

Overview: Teenagers will organize and lead an Advent fair for families.

By sponsoring an Advent fair, teenagers can help make the Advent season more meaningful for themselves and all the families of your church.

To organize an effective Advent fair, have teenagers form several teams. You may want to set up several booths throughout the church, where families can do crafts and projects like the ones listed below. Add your own ideas to this list. Possible teams and responsibilities are as follows:

Facilities and schedule—This team will arrange for rooms, furniture, and other necessary items to be ready on the scheduled day. They'll also plan the schedule for the Advent fair. Please see the box below for a sample schedule.

Sample Advent Fair Schedule

5:00 p.m. Families arrive and share snacks or a light supper.

5:30 p.m. Families are given lists of all of the attractions/booths and are instructed to go to the booths at their leisure.

7:30 p.m. Families come back together for a brief Advent worship time and then are dismissed.

Advent wreaths—This team will be responsible for obtaining all supplies necessary for each family to make its own Advent wreath, including foam or wire rings; evergreen branches; pins or glue; purple, pink, and white taper candles; and ribbons or other decorations. They'll also need to be prepared to explain the process as well as the history and meaning of Advent wreaths. Some excellent resources for this include *The Advent Wreath: A Light in the Darkness* (Augsburg Fortress) and *Before and After Christmas: Activities and Ideas for Advent and*

Epiphany (Augsburg Fortress).

Devotions—This team will help families create their own devotion books for use during the Advent season. These can include Scriptures, songs, and fun family devotion ideas. One great way to create the books might be to give families a list of possible Scriptures, songs, and activity ideas and have them choose the ones they like. Then give them several sheets of paper, and have them write a few ideas on each page. Younger family members can decorate the pages. When the books are finished, have the families three-hole punch the pages and string them together with festive yarn or ribbon.

Advent calendars—This team will help families create their own Advent calendars. Each day will have a fun family activity to complete. Provide a large piece of poster board, markers, and Christmas stickers for each family. Give each family a list of possible fun Advent activities, such as "Go Christmas caroling" or "Have a family game night." Have each family create its own calendar for the Advent season, using your ideas or family members' original ideas.

Refreshments—This team will provide food and drink for the families at the fair. You may want to stick with a Christmas theme.

One Church's Story

"Our church has made this intergenerational Advent fair an annual tradition. We have great attendance at this event, and almost everyone brings the entire family!"

Begin the fair with a welcome and an explanation of the events. The teams can set up in stations, and families can rotate from station to station during the fair. After families have completed the stations, close the fair with an Advent devotion.

Artistic Cover Design

Overview: Teenagers will design covers for worship service bulletins or programs.

Before beginning this activity, explain the importance of worship programs to the group, and encourage them to creatively express their understanding of the Christian faith as they make their designs. As youth create their artwork, remind them that their designs will be used as covers for the bulletins or worship programs in your church.

You'll need blank sheets of paper cut to the size of the church's worship program covers. If you have access to a color copier, the cover designs can be done in color using markers. If the church copier is black and white, use dark markers or pen and pencils to create the designs. If some of the teenagers are reluctant to participate because they think they lack artistic ability, consider letting them work in pairs.

When the designs are complete, arrange for each one to be used as a worship bulletin cover for one week. Consider placing a brief note in the church newsletter or bulletin ahead of time to explain the project and to generate support and excitement.

Variation: You might consider having youth vote on their favorite design and having it printed on T-shirts at a local fabric printing shop.

Fasting Prayer

Overview: Youth will meet together during a meal time to fast and pray for an issue of vital concern to their church.

Do this activity on a regular basis or as a special event when your church is facing a particular concern (such as an emergency health need or the calling of a new pastor). A Sunday after church (missing the noon meal) often works well as a time for a planned fast. Provide juice if you feel that it's appropriate.

Before beginning your prayer time, read Matthew 4:1-2 to remind youth that Jesus set the example for fasting, then read Matthew 6:16-18 to establish the proper attitude when fasting. Depending on the experience and maturity level of your group, you may wish to have the group form pairs or trios to pray for short periods of time while the rest of the group engages in another activity. Another way to organize the fast is to alternate periods of praying with small groups and as individuals, addressing specific aspects of the issue you're praying about through the direction of a leader or at the suggestion of participants.

God can use the exercise of this spiritual discipline as a powerful tool for bonding your youth group to each other and to the church they're praying for.

Invitation Cards

Overview: Teenagers will make printed cards to use in inviting other youth to Christian activities.

Work with teenagers to design printed invitation cards that give information about your church. This idea is one way to make it easy for teenagers to invite others to church activities.

First decide together what size and style you want to make the cards. If you make the cards the size of business cards, they'll easily fit into purses or billfolds. You could also make folded cards like standard invitations with envelopes so youth can sign the invitations and hand them out or mail them.

Then encourage teenagers to come up with a creative design for the cards, keeping in mind the space you have to work with. The cards should include information on standard church services, Sunday school, and youth activities. Include information on days of the week, times, and locations.

You may want to print on the cards, "You are invited to attend one of these activities of our church. You may attend as my guest." When the design is complete, have the cards printed by a professional printing company, and distribute them to your teenagers. Encourage teenagers to use these cards to invite friends to church activities.

Just Clownin' Around

Overview: Teenagers will organize and participate in a clown troupe to share God's message with Sunday school classes, church organizations, and even the entire congregation.

A clown troupe can provide a wonderfully effective ministry for "teenagers" of all ages! Utilize the fun-loving, enthusiastic spirits of your teenagers to create a troupe

of clowns.

First, you'll have to obtain clown makeup from a party supply store or a discount store. Clown costumes can be as simple or as elaborate as you'd like. There are many fun patterns for clown costumes available if you'd like to sew your own, or colorful old clothes from second-hand stores (or parents' closets!) work just as well. You might also like to purchase (or obtain) clown props, such as balloons, confetti, kazoos, beach balls, or old tricycles.

Have each teenager choose a clown "persona." This includes the clown's costume and makeup look and the attitude and possible actions of the clown. (For example, will the clown be happy or sad? Hyper or subdued? Loud or quiet?)

One Church's Story

"Our clown troupe performed at a camp for disabled campers. We acted out several parables and added a whole new meaning to being 'fools for Christ'! The teenagers were very excited about the enthusiastic response they received. And the camp director told the group that some of the more profoundly handicapped campers responded more to the clowns than they had to anything else at camp."

Once you have several clowns established, you'll need to create some brief skits to share with your audience. Christ's parables are great places to start. Two excellent resources for clown skits and other information about clowning are *Clown Ministry* and *Clown Ministry Skits for All Seasons* (both from Group Publishing).

Performance possibilities are practically endless. A clown troupe could perform as part of a Sunday school program or in an individual class, at a nursing home or a children's hospital, at a church talent show, or in a worship service.

On Camera

Overview: Teenagers will form a video team to chronicle the life of the church family.

Teenagers and video cameras can be an amazing combination! Bring out the natural "videographers" in your teenagers with this great ministry opportunity.

Organize a team of teenagers, and encourage them to create a video "yearbook" to chronicle the life of the church family for a specified period of time. (A year would be good.)

Before they get started, brainstorm with the team about the types of things they'd like to include in the video. You may want to have a church calendar available to help with the brainstorming. Some suggestions include large church events, such as a Christmas pageant or an all-church picnic; special worship services; Sunday school classes; mission trips; and even individual interviews. Encourage teenagers to make sure the video is intergenerational and covers a full scope of church activities.

After teenagers have a rough idea of the types of things they'd like in the video, have them create a brief outline and determine who will videotape which events.

Then turn them loose! You may either provide video cameras and tapes, borrow them from church members, or have teenagers use their own. Check in with your video team from time to time to see how the project is coming.

When teenagers have finished their "raw footage," take it to a video editor to edit into a shorter video. (Check around. Video editing companies will sometimes do this for lower cost if they know it's for a church, or a church member may have these capabilities.)

Use the completed video as a fun way to remember the "good old days" in your church. (It also would be a great way to introduce new members to the various ministries and activities your church has to offer.)

Pastoral Encouragement Team

Overview: Teenagers will work to encourage the senior pastor.

Ask some of your teenagers who have the gift of encouragement to join a pastoral encouragement team. Organize your group into the following teams.

• **Worship encouragement**—These teenagers will take notes on the worship service and message. After the service, teenagers should encourage the pastor by sending notes or calling the pastor, referring to specific things they learned from the message.

• **Personal encouragement**—These teenagers will be on the lookout for things that will personally encourage the pastor. Some ideas include giving personal growth books, buying gift certificates, washing the pastor's car, or mowing the pastor's lawn.

• **Professional encouragement**—These teenagers will approach the pastor and ask how they can help the pastor do ministry more effectively. For example, the team might help the pastor think of sermon topic ideas, do research, or plan a worship service. If the pastor is unable to think of any ideas, have the teenagers offer their phone numbers in case anything comes up.

• **Prayer encouragement**—These teenagers will call the pastor and ask for specific personal prayer requests. Then teenagers will pray for the requests. Make sure teenagers know to keep these requests confidential.

Be sure to follow up with your teenagers to see how you can help.

Pizza Box Calling Cards

Overview: Teenagers will follow up with visitors to the church by delivering gift certificates for pizzas.

People may or may not open their door to a church's outreach committee, but they'll *always* welcome a pizza delivery! That's why at a church in Ohio, the visitor follow-up team delivers a pizza box. And it's a perfect place to plug in your teenagers.

Visit your local pizza parlor, and buy gift certificates for medium cheese pizzas. Explain that you'll use them in conjunction with your church. Tell them you'll deliver them to many new people in the community, and offer to buy a dozen at once. You'll get a *great* deal. Get as many clean pizza boxes as you get certificates. You'll need them.

Ask teenagers to develop several written pieces to fit inside the boxes: a letter from the youth group inviting teenage visitors to return, a brochure explaining what the church offers to families, and a letter from the pastor inviting the visitors to return. If your church has a newsletter, include the most recent issue.

Include a supply of "thanks for visiting" letters from the Sunday school teacher for each age level, too. Print out all the letters from a computer, and then have teachers individually sign a stack for use as needed. Editing the letters when volunteer teachers change positions will be easy.

Adapt each pizza box to fit the visitor follow-up call you're making. If the family includes a teenager, put in the letter from the youth group. If there's a second-grader in the family, use a letter from the second-grade Sunday school teacher.

Select a night when your team will make follow-up calls on visitors. Try Tuesday. It seems to be a night most people are home in many communities. At 6:30 or 7:00, show up at the door of a church visitor with the personalized pizza box. Announce that while there's no pizza inside, there *is* a gift certificate for one.

Explain who you are—a team of teenagers who want to invite the family back to church again. Don't press for on-the-spot evangelism. Simply deliver a very memorable invitation. If your team is invited in, it may be an opening to share your faith.

But even if the stunned recipient simply takes the box to look through later, your team has made a *big* impression.

A Christian education director in Michigan discovered that having the senior high youth group make follow-up calls greatly increased the impact of the calls. Visitors thought if *teenagers* were so excited about their faith and about serving the church, something *great* must be happening at the church.

Provide adequate training so teenagers who have the opportunity to share their faith are able to do so. And consider providing adults to drive. You'll reduce the insurance liabilities and offer reassurance when visitors open their doors.

Prayer Chain
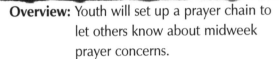

Overview: Youth will set up a prayer chain to let others know about midweek prayer concerns.

Prayer needs don't always happen on Sunday mornings. Help your teenagers set up a prayer chain to stay informed about prayer concerns during the week. Explain that youth who want to pray for others can sign up as prayer chain members. If a prayer concern arises during the week, anyone can call the youth leader. Then he or she will call the first person on the prayer chain list. That person will call the next person on the list, who will call the next person on the list, and so on.

List the names and phone numbers of everyone who wants to be a prayer chain member, and give each member a copy of the list. Ask members to commit to praying for every concern that comes through the chain.

Prayer Visitors

Overview: Students will offer your church a gift of "prayer" for one month of church meetings.

Have one or some of your youth attend the church meetings that happen over a one-month period. Set up a prayer station in each of your church meeting rooms. This should be off to the side of the meeting but within hearing distance.

The students should report to that station during a meeting. Encourage them to be in constant, silent prayer during the meeting. They'll be able to hear what's going on in the meeting, but they shouldn't offer ideas in the meeting. Their only duty is to be in constant prayer.

The pastor, church leaders, and others should feel free to give prayer requests to the students who attend their meetings. This can be done ahead of time or during the meetings. Let the leaders know that the students will be at their meetings solely for prayer support. They should use that prayer support as much as possible. For example, as the Christian education committee worries over a lack of teachers or funding, they should immediately tell the praying teenager about the need. That young person will pray about the need as soon as it arises. Of course, those at the meeting will still spend time in prayer as is customary for that particular meeting.

This can be an important lesson for young people about the powerful effect prayer has in a church when people are willing to meet and work together to accomplish God's will.

Encourage the students to keep journals about the prayer requests. Take some time at youth meetings to discuss the power of prayer and the need for it in church administration. Explain to the students the power they're bringing to a meeting when they're willing to give up their time and go to a meeting to pray. Undoubtedly, this type of prayer support will have a profound impact on the administration of your church programs. It also may cause you to seek the same kind of prayer support during your youth meetings.

Presenting Prayer

Overview: Teenagers will establish a regular time of prayer during the church's worship service.

Most churches' worship services address the concerns of the adults and even the children through children's sermons. But the concerns of teenagers often are forgotten.

If some of your teenagers feel comfortable praying aloud in front of groups, you can help them establish a regular time of prayer in your church's worship service. Not only will teenagers develop their gift of prayer, but all the church's teenagers will feel more included and understood.

You'll have to approach your church leaders about this idea, and you might want to ask one or two teenagers to help you. Teenagers can explain that they'd like to add a new, regular element to the worship service in which a teenager prays about youth concerns. Teenagers also can explain why they think it's necessary and can show enthusiasm, commitment, and preparation—all necessary qualities for the idea to work.

Make sure the teenagers who are interested understand that it will regularly require some extra time from them. They might pray about prayer topics, listen to others' concerns, develop prayers, and practice praying aloud.

First set up a system so teenagers know who's praying every Sunday. For example, teenagers could simply rotate, each praying when his or turn comes again.

To help your teenagers, encourage them to pray about general topics teenagers are concerned about, such as violence or peer pressure. Guide them to avoid specific prayers about youth group members, such as Dave's bad grades or Nicole's breakup. Show them how to use the worship area's sound equipment, and help them practice speaking clearly and loudly enough. Encourage them to speak as themselves instead of trying to sound like the pastor or like they're "supposed to." Regularly give them a few minutes during Sunday school and youth meetings to ask everyone about general concerns. Check in every Sunday with the person who's praying to discuss any concerns he or she might have about the prayer.

Not only the teenagers who are praying, but all the church's teenagers and even the entire congregation will benefit from this special attention to teenagers' prayer concerns.

Rugged Cross

Overview: Youth will create a monument for the church to serve as a reminder of God's incredible blessings.

Have teenagers work together to create a large wooden cross. Explain that there are only two limits on the cross: It must fit in the sanctuary, and the teenagers must pay for all the supplies. Begin by having teenagers come to a consensus on the type of wood to use and the measurements of the cross. Have them sketch out the cross on a sheet of paper. Make sure they decide how the cross will stand up in the church by planning a base for the cross or planning a place to lean it. (You'll want to have teenagers check with church leaders if they want it to become a long-term fixture in the sanctuary).

After the planning is done, have a few teenagers meet at a hardware store to get the necessary supplies. Then have the group work on making the cross together. After the cross is complete, have teenagers bring it into the sanctuary before a church service and place index cards, pens, small nails, and small hammers at the foot of the cross. During the service, have a teenager explain that the youth group has made a cross for the sanctuary to serve as a monument for what Christ has done in the lives of the people in the church.

Have each teenager tell the congregation one thing Christ has done in his or her life, write that thing on an index card, and nail it to the cross. Instruct teenagers to invite others in the congregation to add to the monument before and after each church service. Continue this tradition as long as people are enjoying it.

Sign-Along

Overview: Teenagers will perform during the worship service by singing and signing the words to one or more songs.

Coordinate with the person in charge of your church's praise and worship to see when teenagers can assist with the praise and worship portion of the service. Ask the person which song or songs teenagers can perform with singing and sign language. After you've picked the music teenagers will perform, connect with a person in your community who can teach sign language to your students. (You also can use books on signing, but a live teacher will help your students be much more expressive and interpretative.) Community colleges, public schools, and your own congregation are all good places to start your search for a teacher.

Have the teacher work with your teenagers on the song or songs you've picked. Then have teenagers support the praise and worship portion of your service by performing the song(s) much as a church choir would. If your teenagers are interested in the ministry opportunity, consider having them lead an entire praise and worship session.

Teaching Assistants

Overview: Teenagers will help teachers in children's Sunday school classes.

Teenagers who have a gift for teaching and are willing to devote a few hours a month to developing that gift can be a blessing to the church's Sunday school teachers and children.

Talk with your church's educators about setting up a system in which teenagers serve as assistant teachers. The teenagers shouldn't always miss their own Sunday school class, so it's best to have them split their time between classes. Depending on the system you create, assistant teachers may help teachers prepare the lessons but may be in class only every two or three weeks.

Stress that teenagers want to be encouraged and challenged to use their gifts and so will be helpful and committed if allowed to fully participate. While the assistant would be expected to help with preparation and cleanup, he or she also should actually teach a portion of the class. With that in mind, the assistant teacher could meet with the teacher to go over the lesson. The two could pray together, review the Bible stories, and prepare for the activities. They could meet before class to prepare and afterward to clean up.

Ask for the teachers' help in matching interested students with the right age levels, and meet with the teachers and assistant teachers regularly to receive feedback and to address any problems.

Teaching Confirmation

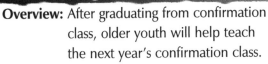

Overview: After graduating from confirmation class, older youth will help teach the next year's confirmation class.

Older youth who have just gone through confirmation often get lost in the shuffle. They're ready to do something besides just attend church services, but often there are few opportunities for them to become involved.

Since these teenagers have just graduated from confirmation, the course material is fresh in their minds. They may need a boost to get them involved in their next phase of church life. Often they're very willing volunteers if asked to fill a valuable role.

Teenagers can share in the ministry of teaching the youth in the confirmation class. And teenage confirmation class leaders can provide excellent role models beyond the adult leaders. Before assigning a teenager to work in this ministry, it's important to make sure the adult leader is comfortable with the shared teaching and committed to helping with the growth of the teenage leader as well as the confirmation class.

One simple way to start involving teenagers is to have them read a Scripture lesson or lead a song or a prayer. They may then move to leading a small-group discussion. Eventually the role can grow to a true shared teaching responsibility, where the co-leaders can plan sessions together and reverse roles from one session to the next. The teenagers may also help some of the confirmation students understand concepts in one-on-one discussions.

The teenagers who lead the sessions will develop skills like these:

- basic leadership skills and the ability to lead activities

- an understanding of how to bring out participation in discussions

- a comfort level in leading prayers

- a comfort level and confidence in being a role model for other youth

• a feeling of value from making volunteer contributions to the church

In addition, the experience will reinforce the truths they learned in confirmation the previous year.

Those Were the Days

Overview: Teenagers will use their own experiences to determine how best to impact the kids in the church.

Encourage your youth to think back to the not-so-distant past, and ask them what would have made church a more meaningful experience for them at a younger age. If you have a senior high group, perhaps they'll want to focus on their time as junior highers in the church. Or maybe your group will use the church's children's program as its focus.

Have teenagers make lists of activities in the church that had positive spiritual impact on them at that age and lists of activities that had little or no spiritual impact. Then have them think about what the church could have done differently to help them in their spiritual growth. Finally have them ask themselves the following question: What's one thing I wish I had learned at church that would have made getting to my current age easier?

Youth may also wish to interview the kids in your church to see if their conclusions about what might help kids in the church actually match what "real kids" are thinking.

When your group has come up with a list of ways to improve children's education or programs in the church, help them choose one thing they can do with the information they've gathered. For example, if your group decided that there should be more sports activities in the children's program, have them host a game day for the kids. If they decided that there should be more field trips, have them take the kids on a quick trip. (The trip doesn't have to be elaborate—just a trip for ice cream with the "big kids" would be enjoyable for the children.)

After your group has planned and carried out its event, have them decide if they'd like to pass the information they've developed on to the director of children's education at your church.

Twenty-Four-Hour Prayer Vigil

Overview: Teenagers will organize and participate in a twenty-four-hour prayer vigil for the church.

This event is appropriate any time during the year, but it has special meaning if incorporated as part of Advent, Easter, Pentecost, or Palm Sunday activities. This activity can be a youth-only activity, or you can invite other church members to participate.

Planning for this event should begin at least two months in advance to allow for sufficient publicity and necessary arrangements. Because of work and school schedules, the best time to plan a prayer vigil of this type is Friday evening to Saturday evening or Saturday morning to Sunday morning and ending just before worship.

> **Tip**
>
> *For added comfort and security during the night hours, consider having two people sign up for each interval.*

As the teenagers begin to plan, they'll probably want to decide on a theme or topic. If the prayer vigil is near a holiday, the theme can be holiday specific. If it's during another time of the year, it might be connected with a special need of the community, a building dedication or project, or simply a time for personal prayer and renewal.

For organizational purposes, encourage teenagers to develop a detailed sign-up sheet that is divided by prayer intervals of approximately thirty minutes.

Here are some things to consider when planning a prayer vigil:

• Choose an appropriate comfortable prayer station within the church where participants are to come and pray. This station might be located in the worship area or sanctuary, a chapel, a church office, or another room set up specifically for that purpose.

• Provide a table at the prayer station for such things as devotional materials, Bibles, pencils, paper, a twenty-four-hour candle, and a clock.

• Develop a list of suggested Bible readings to help participants focus on the theme.

• Make transportation arrangements for teenagers and elderly people if they're involved.

• Be sure to publicize and recruit for the event early.

• Provide participants with a handout ahead of time as a reminder of their commitment and giving simple instructions. (Use the handout on p. 106 or develop your own.)

Twenty-Four-Hour Prayer Vigil

Participant name:

Your day and time for prayer:

Location of prayer station:

Prayer theme:

Additional Instructions:

• Please arrive a few minutes prior to your scheduled prayer time.

• When you arrive, proceed quietly to the prayer station, sit down, and begin focusing on prayer.

• Should you choose to use them, several devotional resources have been provided on a table at the station.

• When your scheduled time of prayer is over, feel free to continue to pray. Or when the next person arrives, feel free to leave quietly.

Visitation Teams

Overview: Youth will visit new teenagers who attend your church.

Organize your teenagers into groups of three, and give them a list of teenage visitors who have attended your church recently. Schedule visitation times one evening each month. Before you go out, refresh teenagers' visitation skills by reminding them of the following.

• Stick together. If one person enters a house, everyone should enter. Never split up and go to separate homes.

• Ask people what attracted them to your church. Ask them what they liked about what they saw.

• Give them a list of upcoming youth activities. Take church literature with you in case they want more information.

• Always leave the church phone number with people. Never offer your home phone number.

After each visitation event, have teenagers return to the church to report and debrief. Be sure to report to your pastor or other church leaders, telling them who you visited.

What God Is Doing

Overview: Teenagers will create a video that demonstrates how God has changed the lives of people in the church.

Give teenagers the task of creating a video that demonstrates how God is moving and working in the lives of people in your church. Have teenagers form various committees to oversee different aspects of creating the video. For example, you may want one group to serve as the directors, one to serve as the scriptwriters, one to serve as the interviewers, one to serve as the editors, and one to serve as the presenters.

Have the directors work with the rest of the group to decide which members of the congregation they should interview. If teenagers don't know who to talk to, have them ask the pastors of your church for direction. Have the scriptwriters create the question(s) interviewers should ask. Then have the interviewers contact the members of your congregation the directors feel they should interview. After the interviews have been collected, have the editors edit the tapes so they're as interesting and meaningful as possible. Some video cameras have editing functions on them, or your teenagers may have access to other editing equipment.

After your group has viewed the edited interviews, have the presenters play the video for the church. If the video is long, have the presenters show one interview each week until all the interviews have been presented.

Youth Prison Ministry

Overview: Generations will minister together to youth in prisons.

Youth prison ministry is done mostly through parachurch organizations that are specifically designed to reach the youth inmate population. It may serve you best to research who is reaching the youth inmate population in your area prior to implementing this program. You may want to obtain information from local area youth services, Prison Fellowship Ministries, and various youth holding facilities in your area. This would allow you to give additional support to an existing ministry and glean understanding from their expertise or join an already established organization that is reaching youth inmates.

Prison ministry is rarely done through a church for several reasons. First, it's difficult for churches to reach a body of people they can't see and interact with on a regular basis. Second, it's often hard to minister to people who have hurt others or who have obvious sin in their lives. Third, it's a ministry that doesn't give back as much as it takes. It's important to recognize, pray over, and talk about all these issues prior to implementing this ministry.

Intergenerational youth prison ministry is important because not many people are doing it and there is a need. And very few youth are involved in ministering to youth in prison. To implement an intergenerational youth prison ministry, you need a strong core of people who have a passion for youth and are committed to ministering to youth inmates. Inconsistent ministering will do more harm than good. Extensive training and commitment are needed for this to be effective. This might work best if these individuals are involved in a small group together or another discipleship time that allows equipping and group growth to occur outside the specific ministry time at the prison.

Place a heavy emphasis on youth leadership. Youth inmates will be more likely to respond positively to committed youth than to committed adults. This doesn't decrease the importance or the effectiveness of adults in this ministry. Adults will provide accountability, wisdom, guidance, and training for the youth.

Here are some examples of specific types of ministry that can be done in youth detention centers:

• **Sports camps**—Have coaches provide guidance in various sports. At the end of the athletic time, offer opportunities to discuss spiritual issues.

• **Care packages**—Have members of your team coordinate a drive to stock care packages. Clothing, magazines, music, candy, and snacks would be greatly appreciated. (Check with the detention center warden to know what is and isn't acceptable to put in the care packages.)

• **Classes**—Coordinate various classes that aren't offered in the prison school curriculum. For example, CPR, art, music/band, health, and various technical/vocational classes would benefit many of the youth.

• **Bible studies and prayer groups**—Offer these activities for those who are interested in learning more about God and growing in their faith.

If you have the resources to effectively communicate the truth of Jesus to youth inmates in your area, this ministry will not only allow those you minister to an opportunity to grow in their faith, it will help your team members grow as well.

Investment-Level Index

Low-Investment Ideas

11, 16, 18, 21, 25, 28, 31, 34, 39, 41, 43, 47, 48,
49, 50, 51, 53, 55, 60, 61, 63, 64, 66, 68, 69, 74,
75, 85, 87, 88, 90, 92, 93, 97, 99, 103, 104, 105

Medium-Investment Ideas

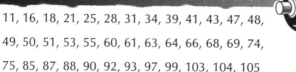

12, 14, 16, 19, 24, 26, 27, 28, 33, 34, 37, 40, 45,
46, 47, 53, 55, 57, 58, 61, 65, 71, 72, 75 76, 77, 83, 89, 94, 95, 96, 101,
102, 107

High-Investment Ideas

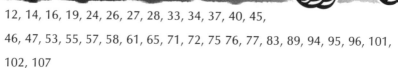

13, 18, 23, 29, 35, 43, 44, 52, 58, 59, 71, 78, 98, 100, 107, 108

Group Publishing, Inc.
Attention: Product Development
P.O. Box 481
Loveland, CO 80539
Fax: (970) 679-4370

Evaluation for *NO MORE US & THEM*

Please help Group Publishing, Inc., continue to provide innovative and useful resources for ministry. Please take a moment to fill out this evaluation and mail or fax it to us. Thanks!

● ● ●

1. As a whole, this book has been (circle one)

not very helpful   very helpful

1   2   3   4   5   6   7   8   9   10

2. The best things about this book:

3. Ways this book could be improved:

4. Things I will change because of this book:

5. Other books I'd like to see Group publish in the future:

6. Would you be interested in field-testing future Group products and giving us your feedback? If so, please fill in the information below:

Name _____

Street Address _____

City _____ State _____ Zip _____

Phone Number _____ Date _____

Bible Study Series

Give Your Teenagers a Solid Faith Foundation That Lasts a Lifetime!

Here are the *essentials* of the Christian life—core values teenagers *must* believe to make good decisions now...and build an *unshakable* lifelong faith. Developed by youth workers like you...field-tested with *real* youth groups in *real* churches...here's the meat your kids *must* have to grow spiritually—presented in a fun, involving way!

Each 4-session **Core Belief Bible Study Series** book lets you easily...

● Lead deep, compelling, *relevant* discussions your kids won't want to miss...
● Involve teenagers in exploring life-changing truths...
● Help kids create healthy relationships with each other—and you!

Plus you'll make an *eternal difference* in the lives of your kids as you give them a solid faith foundation that stands firm on God's Word.

Here are the Core Belief Bible Study Series titles already available...

Senior High Studies

Why **Authority** Matters	0-7644-0892-5
Why **Being a Christian** Matters	0-7644-0883-6
Why **Creation** Matters	0-7644-0880-1
Why **Forgiveness** Matters	0-7644-0887-9
Why **God** Matters	0-7644-0874-7
Why **God's Justice** Matters	0-7644-0886-0
Why **Jesus Christ** Matters	0-7644-0875-5
Why **Love** Matters	0-7644-0889-5
Why **Our Families** Matter	0-7644-0894-1
Why **Personal Character** Matters	0-7644-0885-2
Why **Prayer** Matters	0-7644-0893-3
Why **Relationships** Matter	0-7644-0896-8
Why **Serving Others** Matters	0-7644-0895-X
Why **Spiritual Growth** Matters	0-7644-0884-4
Why **Suffering** Matters	0-7644-0879-8
Why **the Bible** Matters	0-7644-0882-8
Why **the Church** Matters	0-7644-0890-9
Why **the Holy Spirit** Matters	0-7644-0876-3
Why **the Last Days** Matter	0-7644-0888-7
Why **the Spiritual Realm** Matters	0-7644-0881-X
Why **Worship** Matters	0-7644-0891-7

Junior High/Middle School Studies

The Truth About **Authority**	0-7644-0868-2
The Truth About **Being a Christian**	0-7644-0859-3
The Truth About **Creation**	0-7644-0856-9
The Truth About **Developing Character**	0-7644-0861-5
The Truth About **God**	0-7644-0850-X
The Truth About **God's Justice**	0-7644-0862-3
The Truth About **Jesus Christ**	0-7644-0851-8
The Truth About **Love**	0-7644-0865-8
The Truth About **Our Families**	0-7644-0870-4
The Truth About **Prayer**	0-7644-0869-0
The Truth About **Relationships**	0-7644-0872-0
The Truth About **Serving Others**	0-7644-0871-2
The Truth About **Sin and Forgiveness**	0-7644-0863-1
The Truth About **Spiritual Growth**	0-7644-0860-7
The Truth About **Suffering**	0-7644-0855-0
The Truth About **the Bible**	0-7644-0858-5
The Truth About **the Church**	0-7644-0899-2
The Truth About **the Holy Spirit**	0-7644-0852-6
The Truth About **the Last Days**	0-7644-0864-X
The Truth About **the Spiritual Realm**	0-7644-0857-7
The Truth About **Worship**	0-7644-0867-4

Order today from your local Christian bookstore, or write:
Group Publishing, P.O. Box 485, Loveland, CO 80539.